The Valley of Santa Clara

Senator Leland Stanford's Palo Alto Farm

The Valley of Santa Clara

Historic Buildings, 1792–1920

Phyllis Filiberti Butler

With Architectural Supplement by the
Junior League of San Jose

PRESIDIO PRESS

NOTE

Most of the structures listed within these pages are privately owned. Please respect the right of each homeowner to privacy.

In keeping with current stylistic printing practices, accents on Spanish words have been omitted throughout.

First edtion, first printing. Published December 1975 by the Junior League of San Jose, Inc.

Second edition published 1981 by Presidio Press, 31 Pamaron Way, Novato, California 94947

Library of Congress Cataloging in Publication Data

Butler, Phyllis Filiberti
  The valley of Santa Clara.

  Bibliography: p.
  Includes index.
    1. Historic buildings—California—Santa Clara County.   2. Santa Clara County (Calif.)—History, Local.   3. Architecture—California—Santa Clara County.   I. Junior League of San Jose.   II. Title.
F868.S25B8 1981   979.4'73   81-2593
ISBN 0-89141-132-1   AACR2

Preface

Why would Junior League volunteers spend four years and hundreds of hours researching and recording the architecturally and historically interesting structures of this valley? Because this is *our heritage* —yours too—and we need your help to preserve the unique characteristics of our valley and its individual communities, for ourselves and future generations. Since this book's first publication, several important buildings have been razed— most notably the historic Murphy Building of San Jose, the only Civil War era multi-purpose courthouse in the county. Luckily most of the other structures are still standing.

We hope the readers of this book will be as surprised and inspired as we were by the variety and high quality of our architectural heritage. The existence of these venerable buildings, some barely surviving, is largely due to individuals who cared; but we can no longer count on property owners alone to protect our legacy. The cities themselves must act immediately. Each should have its own landmark commission to help define those structures, objects, even trees, that are important to its integrity. Then each should establish methods to ensure continuance of this visible heritage through enactment of local planning ordinances. We need tax relief incentives to inspire the homeowner to protect designated landmarks, and we need agencies willing to finance preservation. Often what we need most is the individual willing to stand up and say, "I care!"

Phyllis Butler cared. A love for old houses and a developing concern for their fate led her to write this colorful study. Her choice of structures was based on five years of intensive research and experience on the Santa Clara County Historical Heritage Commission, of which she was the founding chairwoman. She has conscientiously conducted original research on each structure, taking nothing for granted. This has led her to comb through original deeds, probate files, and trunkfuls of family records. She interviewed scores of descendants, relatives, and present-day occupants of these buildings to acquire first-hand knowledge about the structures and the life that went on in them.

On their part, Junior League volunteers surveyed approximately 1500 buildings, of which more than 350 are included in supplements at the end of every chapter. This listing of additional structures was written and photographed by League members, who dedicated their efforts to the citizens of Santa Clara Valley, in honor of the nation's bicentennial in 1976 and San Jose's own 200th birthday in 1977.

Both the League and the author are very appreciative of the help that has been so generously given by the many individuals, business firms, and institutions that we approached for information about the 426 buildings described in this book. Their names are listed in the Acknowledgments.

We are grateful that over the years this book has helped make historic preservation a vital part of our civic consciousness. If it convinces you that the Valley's fragile architectural heritage is precious and worth preserving, it will have accomplished its mission.

Marilyn Danny Swanson
Julie Rinehart

Publication project coordinators
for the Junior League of San Jose

The Valley

*"It was bloom time of the year . . . The landscapes of the Santa Clara
Valley were fairly drenched with sunshine, all the air was quivering
with the songs of the meadowlarks, and the hills were so covered
with flowers that they seemed to be painted."*

John Muir 1868

From the very first the native Ohlone
Indians preferred this lush vale south of
the San Francisco Bay to the fog laden,
sand strewn stretches of Yerba Buena.

"Llano de los Robles"—Plain of the
Oaks—Portola's scout Jose Francisco
Ortega called it in 1769 as he viewed the
golden, oak dotted expanse from the
skyline ridge. Eighteenth century English explorer Vancouver likened it to
an English park, so dense were the oak
forests then.

It was Father Junipero Serra who was
to give the valley its permanent name
when he consecrated the Mission Santa
Clara de Asis in 1777. The surrounding
pasture lands claimed by the mission
from San Francisquito Creek (at Palo
Alto) to Llagas Creek (at Gilroy) took
on the name and it stuck and was confirmed by the new state legislature in
1850 as Santa Clara County.

The valley had become the domain
of the pleasure seeking, hard riding
"Dons" who ruled over vast ranchos
snatched from the Indians and granted
to them for the most part in the disson-
ant days after the Mission lands were
secularized in the 1830's.

Here came the first foreign settler in
California, John Cameron—alias Gilroy—here Henry Miller centered his
Miller-Lux dynasty. The San Francisco
moguls chose it as the proper setting for
their pretentious estates.

Shortly after the turn of the century a
noted author and traveler summed up
the Santa Clara Valley as a fifty-mile
long garden of fruit and flowers, where
in Spring miles of vineyards and trees
in snow-white blossoms burgeoned
forth . . . "A sight not to be seen elsewhere in the world."

Through the years arrived a procession of merchants, mariners, and saints
—in their turn snatching the land
from the Dons; the railroad kings like
Stanford and Hopkins, quicksilver
kings Barron and Bell, President Herbert Hoover, banking potentate A. P.
Giannini, eccentric James Lick, the
electronic geniuses Lee de Forest and
the Varian brothers—writers like Jack
London, the Norrises, and Robert Louis
Stevenson's widow.

Best of all a host of their houses are
left, extant and exquisite with stories of
pastoral days. I was delighted to find it
so—as I hope you will be.

Contents

Preface   v
Introduction: The Valley   vi

Palo Alto, Mayfield, Stanford   9
Juana Briones De Miranda "Adobe"   12
The Frenchman's Cottage   15
Professor Fernando Sanford's House   18
The Squire House   21
The Seale Cottage   22
The Joseph F. Greer Ranch House   26
The Hoover House   28
Supplement   30

Mountain View, Sunnyvale   35
Rengstorff House   36
The Collins-Scott Winery   39
Supplement   41

Los Altos, Los Altos Hills   43
The Merriman-Winchester Ranch
   House   45
Hidden Villa Ranch   49
Supplement   52

Alviso, Milpitas   55
Jose Maria Alviso Adobe   58
The Higuera Adobe and William
   Curtner Ranch House   60
The Wade House and Warehouse   62
The Tilden-Laine House and Store   65
Supplement   67

Santa Clara   69
The Pena Adobe   72
Mission Santa Clara   75
Fernando Berreyesa's Adobe   77
New Park   81
The Arguello House   84
James Lick's Mansion   86
Supplement   90

Saratoga, Cupertino   95
Hannah McCarthy's Summer House   97
E. T. King House and Pettis Livery
   Stable   99
Paul Masson's Mountain Winery   102
Villa Montalvo   104
Rancho Bella Vista   107

Cupertino   108
Miraflores—Beaulieu   109
Supplement   112

Los Gatos, Campbell   117
Rinconada De Los Gatos Adobe   118
James Lyndon House   121
The McCullagh Estate, La Estancia   122
Campbell   124
The Hyde-Sunsweet Factory   125
Supplement   126

San Jose   131
The Luis Peralta Adobe   133
The Roberto-Sunol Adobe   135
Captain Thomas Fallon's House   137
The Murphy Building   139
The Old Santa Clara County
   Courthouse   141
The Lick Observatory at Mount
   Hamilton   144
The Winchester House   146
Supplement   149

New Almaden   157
Casa Grande   161
The Carson-Perham Adobe   164
Supplement   167

Coyote, Morgan Hill, San Martin   169
Morgan Hill's Villa Miramonte   170
The Coe Brothers' Ranch   172
Supplement   174

Gilroy   177
Henry Miller's Bloomfield Farm   178
Vanumanutagi   182
Chappell-Bonesio House and
   Winery   184
Gilroy City Hall   186
Supplement   188

Acknowledgements   190
Pictorial Credits   190
Bibliography   191
Index   192

"Visitors are always impressed by the beauty of the homes,
embowered in roses and climbing vines and surrounded by grounds
adorned with trees and shrubs."

Mary Bowden Carroll in Ten Years in Paradise *1903*

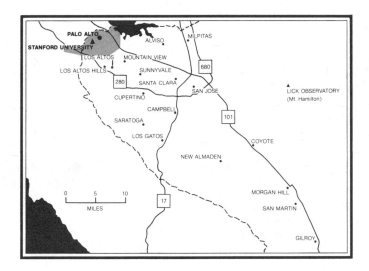

Palo Alto ❀ Mayfield ❀ Stanford

Things must have been a bit crowded, comparatively speaking, along the banks of San Francisquito Creek in the late 1830's. Three families competed for land grants (ranchos) near this important arroyo, the dividing line between the pasture lands of San Francisco's Mission Dolores to the north and Mission Santa Clara to the south. Today the creek marks the northern border of Santa Clara County.

Rancho San Francisquito, which was to become the site of Stanford University, covered nearly 1500 acres from the ancient redwood, El Palo Alto, westward along the creek. It was granted in 1839 by Governor Alvarado to Antonino Buelna, one of four men who led the revolt against the Mexican territorial government in 1836 that put Governor Juan Bautista Alvarado in power.

After the American occupation, Buelna's widow was plagued by squatters who found this area near an old lumber road especially attractive. In 1864, a San Francisco lawyer, who had come into possession of the grant, auctioned it off to Englishman George Gordon who soon built an imposing home there. This is the ill-starred Gordon family fictionalized by Gertrude Atherton in her popular novel of the 1920's, *Daughter of the Vine*. The property was purchased by Leland Stanford in 1876 and became the nucleus of his Palo Alto Farm, taking the name from the rancho deed which had "Palo Alto" tacked on to distinguish it from two other San Francisquito grants.

On the eastern course of the creek was Rancho Rinconada del Arroyo de San Francisquito, the grant on which Palo Alto's original townsite was laid out in 1888. It belonged to Rafael Soto, whose father had been a recruit with Anza's expedition of colonists who

9

The Mayfield Bicycle Club takes a Sunday outing past the Mayfield Hotel on El Camino Real, called Main Street in September 1888 when W. H. Myrick took this picture.

founded San Francisco in 1776. Soto settled on the San Francisquito in 1835. He died before officially gaining title to the rancho but after much difficulty his widow Maria Antonio Mesa received the grant in 1841.

The largest of the three San Francisquito grants was to Lieutenant Jose Pena, a teacher at San Francisco Presidio, who had first settled near Lake Lagunitas in 1824. He apparently expected to be granted the land adjacent to the creek; however, Buelna was closer to the ear of the governor and Pena was forced to move his claim farther south near the present intersection of Alma and San Antonio Road. Pena's Rancho

Rincon de San Francisquito was finally officially granted to him by Governor Alvarado in 1841.

In September 1847 the resourceful Pena, who then was living near Mission Santa Clara (where his adobe town house still stands) sold his rancho for $3,500 to "Don Diego" Forbes who immediately transferred it to the Robles brothers (in exchange for two shares in the famous New Almaden mine).

Teodoro and Secundino Robles were colorful characters given to gambling and high living. Secundino spent thousands enlarging the Pena adobe for his family of 29 children and entertaining at lavish fiestas lasting several days. The Robles brothers soon ran out of funds and began trading off their property on whims.

On part of Robles Rancho near where the lumber route from the hills crossed El Camino Real, Mayfield, the earliest town in the Palo Alto area, sprang up. The little village grew around "Uncle Jim" Otterson's public house built in 1853 on the route of the new county road. The tavern became a stopping place between San Francisco and San Jose, and in 1855 Uncle Jim's Cabin became the official Mayfield Post Office—taking the name from the 250-acre Mayfield Farm nearby.

In 1886 Senator Leland Stanford considered developing Mayfield as the resident village for his proposed university, insisting that it be a "dry" town. The townspeople refused to give up their bustling saloons and breweries, so Stanford looked elsewhere. He contacted Timothy Hopkins, son of his railroad partner Mark Hopkins, and financed him to purchase 740 acres of the Soto rancho. On February 27, 1889, Hopkins filed the subdivision map of University Park.

The new town was not yet called Palo Alto although Stanford's stock farm across El Camino Real was well known by that name. An enterprising real estate developer soon bought 120 acres adjoining Stanford's land on the south from two Mayfield farmers and divided it into residential lots, calling *his* development "Palo Alto." Stanford was furious; he brought suit against the man and an out-of-court agreement was reached whereby the name "Palo Alto" was dropped and "College Terrace" adopted in its place. A few months later Hopkins' University Park was rechristened "Palo Alto."

Palo Alto, stretching from San Francisquito Creek along the Alma Street railroad tracks to Embarcadero Road gained immediate acceptance as a fine place to live. After Stanford University opened in 1891 the professors chose it for their homes, its tree-lined streets reminiscent of eastern college towns. Prominent families from all over the Santa Clara Valley began to move there.

Mayfield on the other hand became the local saloon town for the Stanford students, and though the bar business boomed, the more substantial citizens were concerned at the lack of progress in other fields.

On Sunday, January 1, 1905 Mayfield adopted an ordinance banning saloons. Cautiously, a few tavern keepers opened up, then all did. No arrests were made that day as everyone in town, it seemed, went on a last drinking spree. On Monday, however, those who opened their saloons were taken before the justice of the peace and fined—marking the end of Mayfield's saloons and, it was hoped, the start of a bright future for the town.

But it was too late for little Mayfield. The town never reached the stature of its more affluent neighbor to the north and in 1925 was annexed to Palo Alto. Today Mayfield has lost its unique identity, leaving only traces of its boisterous past in a few decaying old houses left on the side streets off California Avenue and a dozen grander homes in College Terrace.

Juana Briones' house, once a well known stopping-off-place between San Francisco and Santa Clara, has been greatly enlarged through the years; part of the original adobe walls are encased in concrete.

Juana Briones De Miranda "Adobe"*

Old Adobe Road, Palo Alto

Tucked away in the foothills along Arastradero Road, just within Palo Alto's western border stands an old house —part adobe, part frame blended together in a charming manner. Here ac-

tress Marjorie Eaton and her coterie of talented friends and relatives live on a tiny parcel of the onetime 4400-acre Rancho Purísima Concepción.

Under the central section of the remodeled, greatly enlarged residence can be seen clay-like earth forming the foundations of the existing walls— remnants of the original adobe house built in 1847 by Juana Briones, one of the most celebrated women of California's Mexican era.

* State Registered Landmark #524

Rather than being constructed of sun-dried adobe bricks, the original house appears to have been a less common type of adobe called "encajando," in which large redwood timbers were used as corner posts, on each side of which were nailed roughly split redwood boards to form a crib. Into this, chunks of adobe soil were poured and tamped down. Often the whole exterior of this type of structure was then plastered over with adobe mud.

The place looks and feels like Juana's sanctuary should. The grey-washed exterior is protected by a covered veranda tangled with an old wisteria vine. In the living area, the thick, cream-colored walls invite reminiscing over tales of its romantic past.

In 1847 Juana Briones de Miranda moved from San Francisco to Rancho Purisima Concepcion. She was the recent widow of a reportedly wild and irresponsible former soldier, Apolinaro Miranda, who had caused her no little trouble during their stormy marriage of 27 years.

In 1836, this independent, ambitious woman had packed up her entire household and left her husband's adobe near Presidio San Francisco, to pioneer in the unoccupied North Beach area below Loma Alta (Telegraph Hill). It was at North Beach, occasionally called La Playa de Juana Briones, that her ascent as one of the preeminent women in California history began.

She was almost invariably described as a widow in those days—although Apolinaro was still around. The spirited lady brought him before the alcalde (justice of the peace) in June of 1842 and June of 1843 for mistreating her.

Charles Palmer Nott bought Juana's four room house in 1900 and began the first of many years of remodeling. This photograph of a group of people on the porch on the east side of the house, dates from approximately that time.

Further, there was born to the long suffering Juana, Jose de Jesus Julian Miranda in 1837, Maria Manuela de Jesus in 1839, Jose Aniceto in 1841, and Jose Dolores in 1842.

Five years later, Juana and the younger children moved down to Rancho Purisima Concepcion purchased for $300 from Jose Gorgonio, an Indian neophyte who had received the grant in

1840. According to land case testimony, Juana immediately built a large adobe dwelling and several out buildings, and settled in with her entourage.

The last record of the venerable Juana's public life was at the 1884 hearings on the proposed canonization of Father Magin Catala, Mission Santa Clara's saintly priest who had died in 1830. Although she attested to the padre's miraculous powers of extrasensory perception and foretelling of the future, the canonization never took place.

In 1880 Juana deeded her home place and the surrounding 40 acres to her daughter Refugia, then Mrs. Ramon Mesa (her husband was son of neighboring Rancho San Antonio grantee Juan Prado Mesa). The couple lived for a while in the main house with Juana. By 1885 the marvelous old lady, now near 90, gave in to the crippling rheumatism that plagued her and moved to nearby Mayfield where her daughters were living.

Juana died in Mayfield December 3, 1889. Her name is the first entry in the Register at Holy Cross Cemetery in Menlo Park—befitting one of the foremost women of early California.

Charles Palmer Nott, a young man who had come from the East to do graduate work in biology at the University of California and Stanford University fell in love with the old place, in spite of its dilapidated condition. In September 1900 he paid $4,000 for the 40 acres and what he referred to as the "old shack of a house and still older shack of a barn."

By November he had made the four boarded-over rooms comfortable enough to move in. The original building was about 42 feet by 18 feet and one-and-a-half-stories high. Upstairs under the eaves was an attic-storeroom, reached by an outside wooden stairway. Downstairs were Juana's dining room, living, and sleeping rooms.

From this spartan beginning Nott fashioned the captivating country house of today. His marriage in 1903 necessitated some remodeling and additions, as did the birth of three children during Nott's 25-year stay here. By 1908 the house, which had been badly shaken in the 1906 earthquake, was in need of major repairs. The Notts decided to protect the walls by coating the exterior with concrete and then plastering over the interior walls. They then added two wood frame wings—the north wing became the kitchen and formal dining room, the south wing held two large bedrooms. The entire U-shaped structure was (and still is) surrounded by a covered veranda, overlooking a garden courtyard.

What remains of the original house is enclosed in the walls of the main living area where the deep-set windows and Mediterranean simplicity are most striking. The Notts sold the house in 1925 to the Eaton family. Marjorie Eaton could be Juana reincarnate—stately, independent, with an ethereal, spiritual quality. She seems to belong in this wonderful house.

Mayfield storekeeper William Paul is pictured here in front of the little house that he sold to the Mysterious Frenchman Peter Coutts in 1875. It is thought to have been incorporated within the structure that has become known as the Frenchman's cottage.

The Frenchman's Cottage

Escondido Road, Stanford University

The villagers of little Mayfield had never seen the likes of handsome, aristocratic Monsieur Peter Coutts, who swept into Mayfield in the spring of 1875 with a call for "a hundred men—not afraid to work." An army of bricklayers, stonemasons and carpenters were engaged to transform local storekeeper William Paul's farm into a pretentious 1,242-acre estate which this

"Mysterious Frenchman" at first called Ayrshire Farm.

The feverish activity continued with the building of a dozen barns, stables and houses—a dairy, wine cellar and 50-foot-high clock tower. When a crew of Cornish miners began digging a network of irrigation tunnels leading to a brick storage tower two miles away, speculation ran wild. The tower was judged as a prison for an alleged "mad" wife and the tunnels as escape routes for the Frenchman when his pursuers caught up with him.

Peter Coutts brought his invalid wife Marie, his ten-year-old son Albert, five-year-old daughter Marguerite, and their governess Mademoiselle Clogenson to live in William Paul's former two-room house, enlarged into an ell-shaped, Normandy-style cottage of nine rooms, the redwood walls covered with elegant French chintz in a pastel floral pattern.

William Paul, the grand old man of Mayfield (he laid out the town in 1867) was as curious as his neighbors about the reserved but amiable Frenchman who had told Paul little about himself —only that he came from Switzerland, and that he wanted to buy Paul's farm to raise thoroughbred cattle.

Coutts purchased several other parcels of the Robles Rancho (Rincon de San Francisquito) lying near the Matadero Creek. A man of catholic taste, he was taken with the Hispanic flavor of the neighborhood and soon dubbed his spread Matadero Rancho, celebrating its completion with a large fiesta.

The true story of the Frenchman—his identity as Paulin Caperon, a wealthy French banker and publisher of an anti-royalist paper *La Liberte*, who had fled France under an assumed name to escape political reprisals by supporters of Napoleon III—wasn't known until years after Coutts' departure in 1881. In that year he suddenly packed up his family and returned to Europe, leaving the cottage intact. His 1881–1882 correspondence from London indicates he planned to return eventually to Matadero Rancho. When the way was

cleared, Caperon and his family returned to France where he regained the balance of his vast fortune. Eventually he built a magnificent chateau on Lake Geneva. Legend claims it as one originally intended to be built on Matadero Rancho. The Frenchman never returned to California, but in 1926 his granddaughter did, and at Stanford University told the real story of banker-publisher Paulin Caperon, alias "Peter Coutts."

In November 1882, Senator Stanford, whose Palo Alto Farm adjoined on the north, purchased Matadero Rancho for $140,000. It became a center of stock breeding for Stanford's thoroughbred race horses. In 1887 the cottage became the temporary residence of Charles A. Coolidge, one of the architects of the university.

David Starr Jordan, the newly appointed first President of Leland Stanford Junior University arrived at the Frenchman's Cottage with his wife and young son in June of 1891. It was to be their home for three years. They found the cottage "picturesque if not entirely comfortable." Their first afternoon there Senator and Mrs. Stanford came over by carriage to call, and as they sat on the veranda making plans for the new university, Mrs. Stanford told the Jordans tales of the mysterious Frenchman, Peter Coutts, who had built their cottage. Many of the romantic, if erroneous, Frenchman legends apparently began with Jane Stanford and were embellished upon by Doctor Jordan. The inaccurate description of the cottage as a replica of Marie Antoinette's

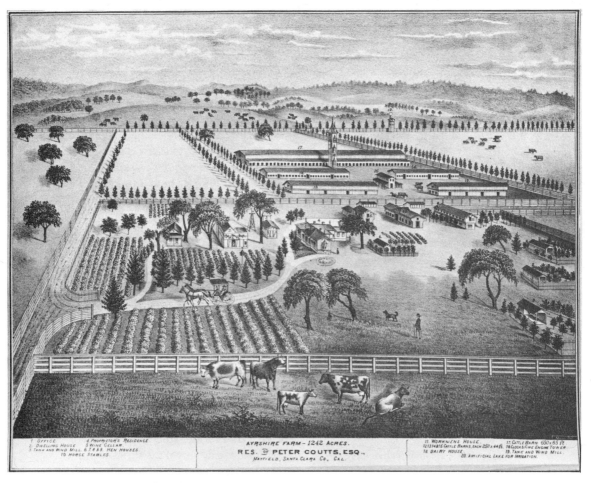

1. OFFICE	4. PROPRIETOR'S RESIDENCE		11. WORKMEN'S HOUSE	17. CATTLE BARN 650 × 65 FT.
2. DWELLING HOUSE	5. WINE CELLAR		12.13.14.& 15. CATTLE BARNS, EACH 250 × 44 FT.	18. CLOCK & FINE ENGINE TOWER
3. TANK AND WIND MILL 6.7.8.9. HEN HOUSES			16. DAIRY HOUSE	19. TANK AND WIND MILL
10. HORSE STABLES				20. ARTIFICIAL LAKE FOR IRRIGATION

AYRSHIRE FARM – 1242 ACRES.
RES. OF PETER COUTTS, ESQ.,
MAYFIELD, SANTA CLARA CO., CAL.

The plan of the Frenchman's 1,242 acre estate which he first called Ayrshire Farm and later Matadero Rancho was included in Thompson and West's 1876 historical atlas. The entire plan was not followed exactly; however, the cottage (in the center of the plan, marked 4) is depicted as it stood until a second floor was added in the 1930s.

Petit Trianon, the story that Coutts had fled France with Alsatian funds entrusted to his bank, and the possibility of the governess being Empress Eugenie, were recounted around the cottage fireplace on chilly evenings to the delight of the Jordans' student visitors.

Dr. Jordan christened the house "Escondite," for "hiding place"—which later became the Spanish equivalent, "Escondido." Down through the years a succession of Stanfordites have made it their home. The ATO fraternity took over after the Jordans moved out in 1894. The ebullient Klondikers, a girls' club of 1898 to 1900, were followed by a chain of professors and their families who added a sleeping porch and a second story to the fabled Frenchman's old cottage. These days it stands enigmatically amid the tract houses of Escondido Village, the University's student housing project for which it is the headquarters.

Fernando Sanford, one of Stanford University's original 15 professors of 1891—dubbed "The Old Guard."

Professor Fernando Sanford's House

450 Kingsley Avenue, Palo Alto

One of the most beloved of Stanford University's pioneer professors was Fernando Sanford, who came to the new campus in September 1891 when, according to him, it was "little more than a hayfield."

Professor Sanford was to head the physics department at the invitation of Dr. Jordan. He was one of the group of 15 professors who launched the fledgling university. Later they were dubbed "The Old Guard."

Sanford left his home state of Illinois, where he had been teaching at Wake Forest University, to take his chances at Stanford, in spite of the eastern press view "that there is about as much need for a new university in California as for an asylum for decayed sea captains in Switzerland." He confessed his interest in the university had been aroused by reports of "big salaries," but Sanford laughingly observed, "they were wrong."

For the first four years, Professor Sanford, his wife Alice, and their children, Burnett and Alice, lived on Alvarado Row on the campus. In 1894 construction was begun on their home on Kingsley Avenue near Waverley Street in the midst of Professorville. The architect, Frank McMurray of Chicago, was a former student of Professor Sanford. He designed the three-story, 14-room frame house with a variety of features fashionable at the time— Queen Anne corner tower, a palladian window in front, and an unusual archway reaching out past the second story. The overall effect is not unlike early Richardson country homes. A comfortable, columned front porch reaches across the front to the west side of the house, where a doorway—once the carriage entrance—has been covered over in later years. The original house plans call for a darkroom in the attic. This was apparently never completed and the discovery by the most recent owners of one of Professor Sanford's notebooks on "colorvision" suggests he did research in a small outbuilding in

Professor Sanford's fourteen room frame house with its Queen Anne corner tower and unusual second story archway looks today much as it did when it was built in 1894, in the section of Palo Alto known as Professorville, so called for the preponderance of Stanford professors who lived there.

back alongside the old barn, now the garage. Burnett Sanford recalls that his father conducted a study of "earth currents" there for many years.

When in 1948 the professor died in his sleep, a venerated sage of 94, only one of the Old Guard who had founded Stanford University survived him. His wife, Alice, had died three years earlier. Burnett and his wife lived on in the house for a while, and then it stood

empty for some time while new owners made plans to refurbish and modernize the interior. The neighborhood children reportedly looked on it as "spooky and haunted," but since 1951 it has been lovingly cared for by its present owners and looks today much as it did when the Sanfords moved in 80 years ago.

The Squire House*

900 University Avenue, Palo Alto

In 1904 when construction of the Squire house was begun Palo Alto was a thriving college town, attracting many new residents with its intellectual aura.

John Adam Squire, son of a wealthy Boston meatpacker, had brought his bride Georgiana west in 1888 to tutor in Latin and Greek at the State Normal School in San Jose. When Stanford opened in 1891, the Harvard-educated Squire moved his family to Palo Alto and enrolled in the university, continuing studies in the classics along with his new-found enthusiasm, meteorology. After their second and third daughters were born, the Squires decided to sell their small house on Emerson Street and build something larger on the quarter-block they owned on University Avenue at Guinda, then at the edge of town.

John Squire hired T. Patterson Ross, a promising San Francisco architect who had already designed a handsome residence on University Avenue for another Palo Alto family. For a cost of $16,000, Ross executed a nearly perfect example of Classical Revival Architecture which used Greek temples as its model. The style which originated in Post-Revolutionary America (but is popularly thought of as Colonial) had first swept the country during the 1830's to

In 1904 John Adam Squire had this nearly perfect example of Classical Revival architecture built on University Avenue.

1860's. Although it was enjoying a revival throughout early twentieth century California, the style was a startling innovation in unpretentious Palo Alto with its rustic cottages and artistic bungalows. In choosing this style for his home Squire reportedly was thinking of his father's home in Boston, but perhaps he had in mind the similarity of Palo Alto to Harvard's Cambridge as a university town. In 1836 it was reported that "the fashion to build country houses in the form of a Grecian temple, with a projecting portico . . . resting on magnificent columns . . . prevails at Cambridge," especially on the continuation of the old turnpike through town. That is exactly what John Squire chose for his home on Palo Alto's "turnpike," University Avenue, eventually to become the main access road into Palo Alto.

The tradition of buildings modeled after Greek temples was begun in the United States by Thomas Jefferson in the Pavilions, which combined classrooms as well as living quarters at the University of Virginia. Pavilion II (built in 1818) especially seems a model for the Squire house with its triangular pediment running the full front width of the portico and its four Ionic columns rising the full height of the building.

The stately mansion was the scene of a continuing round of parties during the three Squire girls' Stanford years. They could entertain "nearly as often as they wanted," Ruth Squire recalls, except on Saturday nights because of early Sunday morning church. John Squire

* State Registered Landmark #857

Mrs. John (Georgina) Squire and two of her daughters are shown in this photograph taken in the 1930s in front of their house.

was one of those God-fearing, gracious gentlemen who seemed especially prevalent in those days.

John Adam Squire died at home in 1930; his widow Georgiana stayed on in the mansion until her death at age 98. The house was sold shortly after in 1959.

In the years following the sale of the house, Palo Alto's growing urbanization pushed the commercial boundaries of University Avenue threateningly close to this unique residence. In 1971 on the eve of its demolition, as so often is the case, history buffs and others who recognized the Squire House's architectural importance banded together and in a year-long effort raised the funds to purchase and save the house, which is now a state registered landmark.

The Seale Cottage

1103 Ramona Street, Palo Alto

No roster of Palo Alto pioneer clans would be complete without the Seale family. A bizarre web of circumstances resulting in the death of three men entangled them before they were able to take possession of much of the land which later became Palo Alto.

A charming two-story redwood shingle cottage sits peacefully on tree-lined Ramona Street, just within the borders of the original townsite that the Seales sold to Timothy Hopkins in

A turn-of-the-century gathering on the grounds of the former Seale Ranch which stood near today's Jordan Junior High School on what was to become the Seale Addition to Palo Alto.

1887. Here Alfred Seale, whose father Thomas owned the nearby large Seale Ranch adjoining Palo Alto, brought his bride, Grace, after their marriage in 1903 at Stanford Church.

By then the dramatic events that took place nearly 50 years earlier, not far from the old Mayfield station south of town, had been all but forgotten by the few remaining old-timers. Thomas Seale and his two brothers, Henry and Joseph, had come to California via the Isthmus of Panama in 1850. The three Irishmen had some success in San Francisco as grading contractors. They claimed to have done the original grading of Montgomery Street. It is said that one day in 1853 Thomas Seale rode his horse down the Peninsula to the Mayfield area in search of Santa Clara Valley pasture lands for his dray horses. Here he met Captain John Greer who was attempting to obtain confirmation on the Soto grant for his wife and her family. When in 1854 their petition to

the U.S. Land Commission was denied, the Soto heirs entered into an agreement with Thomas Seale whereby he would receive half of their 2200-acre Rancho Rinconada del Arroyo de San Francisquito if he was able to somehow persuade the district court in San Francisco to reverse the decision.

Evidently Thomas Seale was a man of some influence because in 1855 the rancho was confirmed to the Sotos and they signed over some 1200 acres to him, including the main house and barns.

A conflict shortly arose over just who owned a certain portion of the grant. A family named Shore had bought a parcel of land from one Soto heir before

This two-story redwood shingle structure is the Ramona Street cottage where young Alfred Seale took his bride, Grace, shortly after their marriage in 1903.

the transfer to Seale and the property remained jointly held with the boundaries undecided.

In January 1859, brothers Richard and Paul Shore began erecting a house on the disputed land. Thomas Seale, believing they had no legal right there, came to their cabin with his hired man determined to eject them. An argument began between Seale and Richard Shore. Paul Shore was standing nearby holding an ax. Meanwhile, Samuel Crosby, a neighbor of Seale's, arrived on the scene with a pistol (he claimed later to have borrowed it from Seale some time earlier). Seale took the pistol from Crosby and ordered Shore to put down the ax. As Seale moved toward him, Paul Shore struck Seale who dropped the pistol. In the scramble that followed Shore was shot and killed.

Thomas Seale rode to San Jose that evening and turned himself in to the sheriff, asking for an investigation of the shooting.

In March, Thomas Seale and his hired man Alexander Robb were indicted at the district court in San Jose. Samuel Crosby had been summoned as a witness. As he approached the courthouse he was hailed from behind by Richard and Tom Shore, another of the five Shore brothers. Crosby turned and a shootout began. Crosby, who was hit immediately, managed to return fire—although none of his bullets hit their mark. An innocent bystander watching the melee from the courthouse steps was killed by a wild shot.

Crosby, on his knees, tried to cock his pistol but the Shores fired several more shots first and killed him. The Shore boys mounted their horses and fled; they never were prosecuted for the killing.

Thomas Seale's trial was transferred to Alameda County and on April 24, 1859 he was found not guilty. But his troubles were not over. The remaining Shore brothers had resolved to "get even" with him. Seale conveyed his property to his brother Henry and went first to the Comstock mines, in Nevada, then on to Australia. It wasn't until 1863 that Thomas Seale returned to California. That year he married Marian Sproule in San Francisco and their two children Alfred and Mabel were born there. He apparently never returned to his ranch until shortly after his brother Henry's death in 1888.

The following year Thomas Seale retired as superintendent of Senator Stanford's California Street Cable Railroad in San Francisco. He reclaimed his property, retaining over 600 acres of the ranch even after the sale to Timothy Hopkins of the future site of Palo Alto. In the large house that Henry Seale had built in 1878 (on the site of the original Soto Rancho near Jordan Junior High School), Thomas's wife, Marian, died just a few months after their return.

The junior Seale's daughters, Barbara and Marian, were born in their parent's Ramona Street honeymoon cottage and played with the other children of Professorville. It seems likely that the builder was Gustav Laumeister, a local contractor who constructed many similar homes in the area. He was married to Alfred Seale's sister Mabel. The house with its gabled roof and six light cottage windows is a comfortable example of the brown shingle Bay Region style that abounds in Palo Alto and Berkeley as well.

Downstairs the kitchen and breakfast room overlook a small rear garden; upstairs are three bedrooms and a bath. The dining room and living room still have the original redwood paneling, although the living room was enlarged by subsequent owners who enclosed the former front porch along Ramona Street.

In 1908 the Alfred Seales built a larger home on Lowell Avenue in the Seale Addition. The cottage was rented to the Reginald McKaig family from Maryland. Since then there have been three owners, all of whom have maintained its original charm.

Joseph Greer's father, Irish sea captain John Greer, who wed the daughter of the Soto rancho grantee.

The Joseph F. Greer Ranch House

1517 Louisa Court, Palo Alto

The Greer clan, as well as the Soto family from which they descend, are all but forgotten in Palo Alto. So dominated is the city's history by Stanford University and its professors, when the huge old Greer house at El Camino and Embarcadero was torn down in 1952 to make way for Town and Country Village, it appeared the last vestige of the Greer/Soto influence disappeared with it.

Not so. Half hidden by the tract houses surrounding it is the large farmhouse of Joseph F. Greer whose grandfather, Raphael Soto, settled on San Francisquito Creek in 1835, and whose grandmother, Maria Antonio Mesa (de Soto) was the official grantee of Rancho Rinconada del Arroyo de San Francisquito.

The Greer house, built in 1905 of lap redwood over pine frame, has a timeless quality about it. Rather than Victorian era gingerbread, it has touches of the more simple Classical Revival, which was popular once again around the turn of the century, with its elongated windows, simulated masonry and wooden window and door trim, as well as its hip roof with attic dormers. After the Greer family's adobe homestead in Woodside was partially destroyed by the 1906 earthquake, some windows, stair raillings, and beautiful beveled glass doors were transferred to this house, which stands just off of Newell Road, the original Embarcadero Road leading to an old crossing of San Francisquito Creek.

In 1905 Joseph Greer built his 14 room ranch house on land that had been in the family of his mother, Maria Luisa Soto de Coppinger Greer, since 1841.

Joe Greer and his wife Mary Haley, whose anniversary barbeques were a popular early Palo Alto/Mayfield affair, loved ranching, riding, and firearms, and the house reflects it. A huge tackroom with hayloft opening high above the ground takes up a large part of the upstairs. But there are elegant details throughout the 14-room house, evidence of the Greer affluence with a built-in, glass-front cabinet in the large dining room; the study walls which were originally trimmed in gold leaf; heavy, carved mahogany panels in the main hallway; and the massive mahogany bannister and newel post. A unique touch are the three plaster of paris frescoes depicting scenes from King Arthur's days affixed to the walls. Joe Greer bought them from an exhibit at the 1915 Panama Pacific Exposition in San Francisco.

The land on which Joseph Greer built his house has been owned by members of his family for more than 140 years. Fortunately, the fine old house has been spared in the often blind progress of Palo Alto's phenomenal growth, and remains an important link with its historic past.

President Herbert Hoover and his wife, Lou Henry Hoover, here with two of their grandchildren on the terrace of their Stanford home, are welcomed back to California in November 1932 following Hoover's loss to Franklin Delano Roosevelt.

The Hoover House

623 Mirada Avenue, Stanford

This interesting and unusual house, which conveys the mood if not the strict architectural elements of Pueblo cliff dwellings, is situated on the crown of San Juan Hill in the midst of the Stanford University campus. For many years it was the residence of President Herbert Hoover and his family, for the most part before he took office as President of the United States in 1929 and for a few years following his defeat in 1932 by Franklin D. Roosevelt. It is now used as the residence of the university presidents.

The huge multilevel house was presented by President Hoover to the university following the death of his wife in 1944, and named in her honor The Lou Henry Hoover House. From the memoirs of architect Birge M. Clark, it is clear why President Hoover found the house an appropriate memorial to his wife—she had a hand in the design of the building from its beginning in 1919 through its completion in the summer of 1920. In 1919, Birge Clark, then a young veteran of the First World War, returned home from serving in the Army Air Force to find that his father, Professor A. B. Clark, had undertaken the design of a new home for the Hoovers, longtime friends of the Clark family.

The Hoovers had just returned to Stanford from several years of traveling throughout the world, most recently in Europe where Herbert Hoover had served as Chairman of the Commission for Relief in Belgium as well as head of Relief and Reconstruction in war-torn Europe for the United States government. The Hoovers both were alumni of Stanford University.

Throughout their nomadic life the Hoovers considered Stanford their home and after 1912, when he was appointed a Stanford Trustee, they spent several years in rented houses in and around the university. After World War I they decided to build their own residence on San Juan Hill amid the faculty homes at Stanford. Lou Henry Hoover had asked Professor Clark if he would take over the design of the house; they had just dismissed one architect whose plans were too grandiose for the Hoovers, who wanted something unpretentious in keeping with the other homes in the area. As head of the Art Department at Stanford, Professor Clark felt he would not have enough time to do the complete design, but said

if Mrs. Hoover would "act as architect" he would supervise and hire a skilled draftsman to do the plans. The major part of the exterior and basic design work had been completed by Charles Davis, former head draftsman for the prominent San Francisco architect Willis Polk, when Birge Clark joined the design team in 1919. According to Mr. Clark, Charles Davis found Lou Henry Hoover, of whom he was quite in awe, "a unique client in all his experience."

Although the Hoovers apparently did not want the house related to any historic style, the interior is decidedly English in character, perhaps unconsciously due to the Hoovers' residence in England. Because the Hoovers loved to look out from high places across the Santa Clara Valley to San Francisco Bay, all of the rooms on the main and upper floors open onto terraces built on the flat roofs.

The 15-room house was completed by the summer of 1920, and Mr. and Mrs. Hoover and their two sons, Herbert, Jr. and Allan, moved in some months before Hoover's appointment as Secretary of Commerce in the Harding Administration. They were in residence off and on during the next eight years. The boys lived here while attending Stanford. On the night of Herbert Hoover's overwhelming victory in the 1928 election the president-elect received the news here at the house. Both of the Hoovers died in New York City—Lou Henry Hoover in 1944, President Hoover in 1964.

The cornerstone reads 1901 on the splendid wooden Gothic Revival St. Thomas Aquinas Catholic Church at Homer and Waverly Streets.

The Downing house at 706 Cowper Street *shows evidence of our "fragile heritage" and the constant threat of destructive forces such as fire and neglect.*

Supplement

Palo Alto ■ Mayfield ■ Stanford

Palo Alto

"Old Palo Alto" has been characterized by the Palo Alto AAUW in its booklet, *Gone Tomorrow?*, as an area of "neat cottages" and "handsome residences." Typical of the old town area around University Avenue are: the elaborately detailed, small 1893 Rosebrook cottage at **225 Emerson** and several large-scale Queen Anne structures, such as the 1897 Delta Tau Delta fraternity house at **707 Bryant** and the 1894 Downing house at **706 Cowper**, recently burned and neglected, but an architectural fantasy of the Victorian age. The 1894 Decker house, now adapted for commercial use, is an eye-catching relief among the modern block structures that surround it at **510 Waverly**. Small turn-of-the-century neighborhood grocery stores are rare in Santa Clara Valley, and it is easy to see why Palo Altans cherish the false-front wooden Channing Market at **532 Channing**.

Some of Palo Alto's impressive mansions were built outside the city limits. Prior to the Squire House, T. H. Goodman built his Dutch Colonial in 1897 at **509 Hale**. The substantial W. D. Tobey residence of "concrete over out-sized beams" was built next door in 1904 and is now **567 Hale**.

The angled streets past Middlefield define the area called Ashby's Addition. Notable here are the elegant Queen Anne-style towered and gabled 1896 Herzinger house at **1023 Forest** and the modest 1897 Peterson cottage at **1110 Hamilton**.

Two houses in the Evergreen Park tract, which opened in 1904, have special appeal. The steeply pitched and gable roofed house at **390 Leland** is richly decorated and a good match for a small Queen Anne tower down the street at **250 Leland**.

Professorville

Timothy Hopkins subdivided land for Senator Stanford in 1889 to provide homesites for the professors who preferred to own rather than lease university land. The area which came to be known as *Professorville* is generally considered to be limited to Kingsley, Lincoln, and Addison Avenues and the cross streets Ramona, Bryant, and Waverly. However, the area's subtly modulated eclectic architecture, clothed in brown shingles with gambrel roofs, is common for several blocks around. Classic examples are Professor Angell's home at **1005 Bryant** and the Bernard Maybeck designed "Sunbonnet House" at **1061 Bryant**. Art professor A. B. Clark designed the stately **433 Melville** house for Professor Charles Gilbert, one of Stanford's first teachers and a leading citizen of Palo Alto. The 1893 Chandler house at **356 Kingsley** demonstrates the area's most appealing restoration effort.

Old Mayfield is defined by streets between California and Page Mill Road, east of El Camino Real. An established settlement many years before Stanford and Palo Alto were founded, Mayfield has little visible evidence of its fine heritage left today. Across El Camino Real, west on California and College, are the streets named for famous universities, all part of *College Terrace* which was subdivided in 1888. Many charming houses may still be seen in these neighborhoods. The imposing Kee home at **2310 Yale** is thought to be the area's oldest structure, dating from 1888. One of Stanford's original faculty members, Latin professor Walter Miller, built the large, handsome home at **2275 Amherst**. Art professor A. B. Clark, who designed many Palo Alto homes, built a simple frame structure for his residence at **2257 Hanover**.

Stately Dutch Colonials dominate three blocks of Kingsley Street. *Joseph Hutchinson, who was chairman of Palo Alto's first governing board built this house at* **433** Kingsley; *Professor Fluegel's house at* 501 Kingsley *was built in 1897 and was said to house an 8,000-volume library. The symmetrical Colonial Revival at* 334 Kingsley *was owned by Professor Slonaker.*

Design of 1906 house built for Theophilus Allen at **601 Melville** *resembles the work of architects Charles and Henry Greene, noted for their medievalized redwood style.*

The Stanfords built this winery in 1883 to process the grapes grown in their nearby vineyards. Adapted later for use as a dairy, a student center, and now a commercial complex, the "Old Stanford Barn" on Quarry Road *has been remodeled several times, but it still retains its simple lines and brick exterior.*

Stanford University

In 1887 Leland and Jane Stanford laid the cornerstone for a university to be built on their 7,200-acre farm in memory of their son. A 28-year old Boston architect, Charles Allerton Coolidge, drew plans from an original quadrangular layout designed by F. A. Walker, F. L. Olmsted, and Stanford. The master plan called for a complex of low buildings, built around an open court with interrelated arcades. The resulting plan was a "first" in the West, with its European formality and symmetry, its heavy Romanesque style, a near copy of H. H. Richardson's work, and its use of connecting arcades in the manner of the California Missions. The Inner Quad, Encina Hall (the men's dormitory), and three engineering buildings were the first to be built. Coolidge also designed the Outer Quad and the Church, Jane's memorial to her husband, but these were constructed in 1903 by Percy and Hamilton from San Francisco, who designed and built Roble Hall (the women's dormitory), and the Museum, constructed of masonry embedded with railroad rails. Following the 1906 earthquake, many of these structures had to be rebuilt. Other pre-1920 buildings include the sandstone Chemistry Building, Student Union, and the Art Gallery.

Prior to the Hoover home, "The Knoll' was planned to house university presidents. Ray Lyman Wilbur lived here from 1918

The 1870 "Red Barn" on Fremont Road *was once the center of a large stock farm where trotting horses were bred and trained for Leland Stanford. It was here that Eadweard Muybridge conducted his famous experiments in filming motion from 1878–79, utilizing a battery of 24 cameras, activated by trip-wires, to film a running horse.*

until 1943 in the Spanish-Gothic structure on **Lomita Drive**, designed by Louis C. Mullgardt. It now houses the university's music department.

In the 1890's the university leased out land near the completed Quad for staff housing, a practice that continues to this day. Since many of the staff members were from the East and Midwest, some of their homes reflected styles common to those areas—but always with the powerful overlay of Bay Area shingle and native wood forms. **Alvarado Row and Salvatierra Street** have fine examples of this period. The large frame J. B. Cooksey house (1900) at **550 San Juan** became the Phi Kappa Psi fraternity house and is now the Stanford Children's Center. Santa Ynez and Dolores Streets contain many brown shingle residences, commonly built after 1906. Outstanding are the 1908 Hempl-Storey house at **739 Santa Ynez**, the neighboring structure at **740**, and the home of E. O. Elliott, Stanford's first registrar, at **756 Santa Ynez**. Across the street stands the fine stucco-half-timbered-shingle Fairclough home, from the period after 1912.

The symmetry and imposing proportions of classical Colonial houses is evident in the two-story portico designed by C. E. Hodges, Stanford's resident architect, for the Orrin Dunns. Built in 1899, the Dunn-Bacon house is located at 565 Mayfield.

A railroad spur was specially built to bring sandstone blocks from Levi Goodrich's quarry in south San Jose to the construction site for the massive, Romanesque arched structures of the Quad.

"There is scarcely a house without an orchard, large or small, while vegetables are raised in great variety and profusion."

J.P. Munro-Fraser 1881

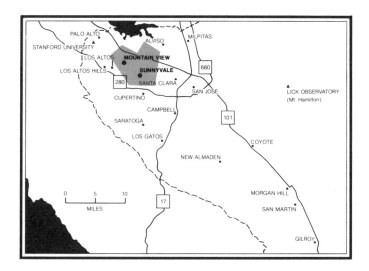

Mountain View 🎴 Sunnyvale

Another town was destined to spring up along the new San Francisco-to-San Jose Stage Road, as today's El Camino Real was known in 1852. That year, James Campbell established a stage stop near the crossroads of the Alviso Road, just a half mile west of where California's first stagecoach line had been pioneered by John W. Whisman in the fall of 1849. Nearby stood the Fremont House, an inn mentioned in many early pioneers' diaries and so well known that the entire Palo Alto-Mountain View-Los Altos area was officially named Fremont Township when the county was first organized in 1850. Across the way from Campbell's Inn, storekeeper Jacob Shumway is reported to have looked across the valley to the mountains and poetically dubbed the spot where they stood "Mountain View."

This scene took place on part of the former lamb pasture of Santa Clara Mission Rancho Pastoria de las Borregas, two square leagues of land granted to Don Mariano Castro's family in 1842. The Castro holdings stretched over six miles along El Camino Real to Lawrence Station Road.

For many years the village of Mountain View was a busy station on the Butterfield Stage Line, but when the San Francisco-San Jose Railroad was opened in 1864 the train route lay a mile northwest of the old town. By the time the railroad was completed, Don Mariano's son Crisanto Castro, had a new town laid out on their lands adjoining the depot which stood near where it does today at the foot of Castro Street. The center of activity began to shift to "New" Mountain View; however, well into the 1890's "Old" Mountain View was the more prosperous location.

The southeastern half of Castro's Rancho Pastoria de las Borregas had been purchased in 1849 by Martin Murphy, Jr., eldest son of the large Murphy clan who helped bring the first

35

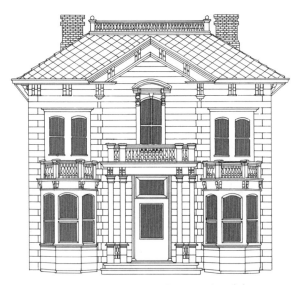

The once elegant Rengstorff House now boarded up stands on Stierlin Road, old Bay Road, in Mountain View.

Rengstorff House

1737 Stierlin Road, Mountain View

Standing in eerie silence in the South Bay marshlands is the Henry Rengstorff residence, onetime showplace of a prosperous German immigrant. Its windows now boarded up, this Italianate structure with a widow's walk and classical columns has been vacant since 1961—a ghostly reminder of its past.

Henry Rengstorff was just 21 when the ship that had brought him 20,000 miles around the Horn dropped anchor in San Francisco Harbor. It was the fall of 1850 and the port was awash with ships abandoned by gold-hungry crews. Rengstorff didn't join the search for gold. Instead, fresh off the schooner, he went to work aboard the Bay steamer *Jack Robinson*, plying between San Francisco and Alviso. Noting the feverish activity at the landings scattered about the Bay, the shrewd German saw where his future lay. Within the decade he had saved enough of his wages to buy two farms and put up a warehouse and store on the Bay marshes near Mountain View.

wagon train across the Sierra in 1844 and eventually controlled six of Santa Clara County's largest ranchos. In his *Americans and the California Dream,* Kevin Starr characterizes the Murphys as ruling the Santa Clara Valley like ancient Irish Kings.

After Martin Murphy, Jr.'s death, his 4,894-acre Bayview Farm (commonly dubbed "Murphy's Station" for the flagstop on the railroad) was divided among his many children. In 1898 real estate developer W. E. Crossman bought 200 acres of orchard land adjoining the old Murphy homestead from Patrick Murphy and subdivided it into lots for the town. At first Crossman called the place "Encinal," but in 1901, due to confusion with an East Bay community of the same name, "Sunnyvale" was adopted. Today it covers nearly 20 times the original town site which was then centered around McKinley and Murphy Avenues.

The flower bedecked living room of the Rengstorff house decorated for Elise Rengstorff's wedding to William Haag in 1889.

By 1860 Rengstorff Landing was the major shipping point for the enormous stores of grain raised in the west side of Santa Clara Valley. The enterprise continued to be successful in spite of strong competition from the San Francisco-to-San Jose Railroad after 1864. That year Rengstorff purchased his third parcel of land, 164 acres that he called his "home farm." Here he had built his somewhat eclectic version of an Italian villa, the fashionable choice of the 1860's and 1870's. His official biography of 1888 notes that the then affluent Rengstorff came to this country ignorant of its manners, customs, and language with only the customary $4.00 in his pocket. From his biography we also learn that in building his "commodious residence representative of the era . . . nothing necessary to comfort that money can procure" was lacking.

Rengstorff and his wife, Christina, raised six children in their spacious home built only three-quarters of a mile from his busy landing. The girls, Marie, Helena, Elise, and Christina, were educated at Mills Seminary. As befitted young ladies of their set, a room was kept at home just for their personal dressmaker who came regularly to outfit them in the latest fashions. The boys, John and Henry, attended Washington College, a short-lived private school of some note in the East Bay. The Rengstorffs had "arrived."

Before the turn of the century Rengstorff owned six ranches in the area, all of which he rented except for the home place. To work the ranch he hired 10 to 12 hands who lived in a large bunk house near the family home. Only the old water tower and pumphouse remain from that era. In his last years Henry retired and Henry Junior managed the landing. John was off in the Klondike, and the girls were all married to upstanding young men.

Henry Rengstorff died at home in 1906. Soon after his death his widow was joined by her daughter Elise Haag and Perry Askam, the orphaned son of her daughter Helena. The young boy grew up on the ranch working in the grain fields and tending cattle while attending local schools and the University of Santa Clara.

Perry was studying music in Europe when World War I broke out. He joined the French army, transferring to the American Ambulance Corps after the United States entered the war. When the war was over he landed in New York and pursued a musical career, appearing in Broadway shows in the early 1920's. His 1927 role as the Red Shadow in *The Desert Song* was at the time rated a classic in the American musical theater.

In 1945 Perry Askam and his wife Frances returned to the Santa Clara Valley to stay with his 83-year-old aunt, Elise, whom Perry considered a second mother. Between concert appearances with the San Francisco Symphony Orchestra Perry lived in his boyhood home until 1959. Since his death in 1961 neighbors and tenants of the house have reported mysterious noises—

Angelia Collins-Scott produced her prize winning wine and brandy in this charming brick building, a one time distillery built in the 1880s and now converted to a home.

crying in the night, doors inexplicably opening and uncanny cold draughts—signs of the "Rengstorff ghost."

The Newhall Development Company, which purchased the Rengstorff ranch in 1953, has been open to ideas for preservation of the mansion. The house was nearly dismantled and moved to Pescadero in the summer of 1972, a plan which fortunately never materialized. Plans for preservation of the Rengstorff mansion have been brought to the Mountain View City Council several times but nothing has been done. Funds have been pledged by the County Historical Heritage Commission to move it to the city's 540-acre Shoreline Park on the site of Rengstorff's Landing. If the City of Mountain View agrees to the relocation, the house would be an appealing reminder of the town's early days—as well as being Mountain View's last important historical landmark.

The Collins-Scott Winery

775 Cascade Drive, Sunnyvale

Stories about old buildings are often hard to believe—the one about this place being an old winery, in particular. There it is, in the midst of the suburban tract homes that are typical of Sunnyvale's look-alike sprawl. It doesn't even appear *old* until you really examine the aging brick. The dormer windows were obviously added on long after Mrs. Scott had her prize-winning brandy stored here in the 1890's.

But the story is true. This comfortable large house is all that's left of the 320-acre Collins-Scott vineyards and winery operation first established in 1880. Salvin P. Collins and his brother, Lemuel Perry Collins, were both born in

New York and came to California in the early 1850's. Lemuel came to the Santa Clara Valley to farm, while Salvin became a partner in a San Francisco saloon. His place on Montgomery Street, with its elaborate mahogany bar was a favorite watering spot for San Francisco business tycoons like James Fair and Alfred (Hog) Davis, president of Fair's South Pacific Coast Railroad.

After Lemuel died in 1879, Salvin took over the 320 acres of orchard which Lemuel had purchased in 1862, and planted 160 acres in vines. In a few years he had built a four-story brick winery and the two-story brick distillery that survives today. It was not uncommon for San Francisco saloon proprietors to have their own vineyards —sort of a private stock supply for their customers. By this time Collins Saloon was also an elegant "Chop House" where Salvin served "fine wine and liquors." Then in 1884, he died.

Salvin Collins' widow, Angelia Russell Collins, whom he had married in 1857, took over the winery operation. By 1889 Angelia had further improved the Collins property. There was a private rail line running through the winery out to the vineyards. She was shipping more than 300 gallons of wine a day—carried by four-horse team wagons—to Jagel's Landing on the Bay at Mountain View.

In 1890 the capable widow had become the wife of Emerson Wesley Scott, a San Francisco importer, who assisted her in running the wine business, which at this time they called the Pebbleside Vineyards and Wineries. Mrs. Scott apparently had also improved the quality of her products; she was awarded first prizes for her "petit pinot" and Zinfandel at the 1894 Midwinter Fair in San Francisco, and was referred to as "one of Santa Clara County's well known wine makers" in a contemporary guide to "Wines and Vines of California." Her time was divided between a home at the vineyard and a house in San Francisco. But by 1896 she was again a widow and resumed full management of affairs from her San Francisco office where she acted as a dealer in wine.

After Mrs. Scott's death in 1897 the property was rented out by her estate. In 1901 an auction was held and all the furnishings and equipment were sold. The dreaded phylloxera (a plant louse that destroys wine roots) had hit the Santa Clara Valley and forced dozens of wineries to close down. The Collins-Scott place survived many changes of hands and periods of neglect while the 320 acres were carved up through the years. The railroad tracks remained until the 1960's. Now all that's left is the brick winery-distillery, converted into a comfortable home.

Supplement

Mountain View ■ Sunnyvale

In Mountain View, the grid of streets between El Camino Real and Evelyn on either side of Castro is graced with numerous, simple frame structures, nearly all built after 1900. Typical are well maintained homes at **322 View and 340 Palo Alto**, both built after 1910. The Pacific Press boarding house, built in 1904 to house female employees, is still standing at **1450 Villa**. Two simple but noteworthy bungalows stand at **1025 and 1043 Villa**. The W. L. Camp house at **336 Mariposa** was built in 1908 by the founder of Mountain View's first bank.

Sunnyvale benefited from the 1906 earthquake by luring industries with the promise of free land. First came the Joshua Hendy Iron Works in 1907, now owned by Westinghouse, on **Hendy Avenue**; this was soon followed by the Jubilee Chicken Incubator Co., now the Brandt Company, at the corner of **Evelyn and Sunnyvale**. In 1908, Libby, McNeil & Libby began operations on **California Avenue**. The original cannery grew into a great sprawling complex, but now only cans fruits and nectars.

The fine old ranch houses are rapidly disappearing from the northern end of the Valley. One handsome holdout is the William Wright house at **1234 Cranberry**, which was built in the late 1860's or early 1870's and was remodeled in 1918.

A stand-out among early industrial buildings, the 1904 Madison & Bonner Dried Fruit Packing House, later California Packing Co., and now Del Monte Corporation, stands at the corner of Evelyn and Sunnyvale.

The deserted frame house and tank tower, surrounded by Navy housing at Moffett Field, was built in the 1850's by Jonathan Richardson, soon after he arrived in California. It was used as a dairy ranch house for many years and was owned by the Theuerkauf family after 1912.

"This part of the country slopes gradually from the bay to the foothills, and here are planted large tracts in vineyards. On every side are seen beautiful homes."

Mary Bowden Carroll 1903

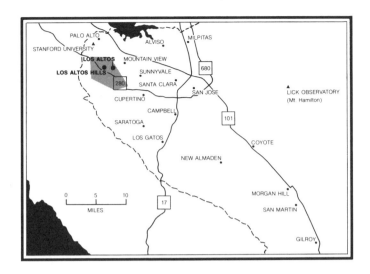

Los Altos ❋ Los Altos Hills

For nearly forty years Mountain View and Mayfield were the only towns in the northern part of Santa Clara County. The wooded foothills belonged to a relatively few farmers who raised grain or planted orchards and vineyards.

The advent of Stanford University and Palo Alto changed the tempo of life amid the sleepy hillsides and in 1906 Southern Pacific began laying double tracks for both a steam railroad running past Stanford University through the foothills to the Santa Cruz resort area, and a suburban electric line by way of Mayfield past Stanford and Cupertino to the west side of the valley.

Southern Pacific executive Paul Shoup, head of the electric line and later President of S. P., spotted a likely townsite on a poppy-covered plateau along the tracks. With several friends he organized the Altos Land Company which purchased 100 acres of the

former ranch of Sarah Winchester and her sister Isabelle Merriman, which lay outside of any rancho boundaries on government land. Their "choice suburban residential section" was at first to be called the unlikely name of Banks and Braes.

In 1908 after the railroad began service, a Sunday barbecue was held for prospective buyers; sales were brisk those first years. (Paul Shoup and his associates by then had wisely changed the towns name to Los Altos, Spanish for "the heights.") Shoup himself had built a typical California shingle bungalow on University Avenue. Just across the tracks lay the business section

43

Juana Briones' house and outbuildings, headquarters of the 5,000 acre Mexican grant Rancho Purisima Concepcion, shown here in 1901.

Mesa's Rancho San Antonio. His fort-like adobe house and corral stood on a knoll southeast of El Monte Road over-looking Adobe (San Antonio) Creek. Mesa, onetime Commander of San Francisco Presidio and a noted Indian fighter received his rancho in 1839. He had attempted to extend his boundaries beyond Adobe Creek to Matadero Creek in the north, totally ignoring the Indian Gorgonio's Rancho Purisima Concepcion.* However, during the land hearings in the 1850's the United States courts upheld Gorgonio's claim to the land north of Adobe Creek, and Rancho Purísima Concepción was approved and patented to Juana Briones, succes-sor to the Indian's ranch.

Part of Rancho San Antonio and near-ly all of Purisima Concepcion make up the wholly residential town of Los Altos Hills. In 1956 a group of residents of the lush, rolling foothills surround-ing Los Altos were understandably concerned as they saw the valley's ranches and orchards become sites of housing tracts and shopping centers. They decided to incorporate with res-trictions guaranteeing a minimum of one acre residential zoning and no commercial development at all.

Isolated and expensive Los Altos Hills has managed to preserve some of the pastoral setting from the days when it was the realm of the Taaffe family who held 2,800 acres just north of Adobe Creek, purchased from Juana Briones by Martin Murphy, Jr., for his daughter Eliza-beth Murphy Taaffe.

along Main Street where his brother-in-law Albert Robinson ran the grocery store in Paul Shoup's building. Near-by was the combination post office and hardware store. Los Altos was on its way.

Contemporary Los Altos has spread across El Monte Road and the Foothill Expressway (which closely follows the old railroad right-of-way) onto Prado

* See Juana Briones de Miranda Adobe, Chapter 1.

The Merriman-Winchester Ranch House

Edgewood Lane, Los Altos

Probably no other residence in the Santa Clara Valley is more of a woman's house than this charming two-story frame structure. It is best known as the oldest house in Los Altos, but its history dates much further back than previously imagined, and women figure largely in its past.

The present owners called in an architect to look the house over with an authentic restoration/remodeling job in mind. When the architect, a conservative New England man, an expert in architectural history, started analyzing the many periods represented in the house—solid brass New Haven, Connecticut hardware dating from the 1880's, an Italian marble fireplace that is unmistakably 1860's, and rough-sawn redwood walls in the library (possibly from the early 1840's he thought)—he realized there was something special about this house.

It became clear that when millionaire Sarah Winchester* purchased this property in 1888 for the use of her younger sister, Isabelle Merriman and her family, rather than tear down an existing structure, it was added onto. An earlier one-and-one-half-story gabled roof

Philanthropist Isabelle Pardee Merriman.

---

* See Winchester House, San Jose, Chapter 8.

The Merriman-Winchester Ranch house, Los Altos' oldest structure, may date back to the mid-1800s.

house was joined with the much larger two-story 1888 portion which makes up the front and east side of the present building.

The earlier house was occupied from 1872 to 1885 by Julia H. Miller Van Reed, her husband James, and their daughter Margaret. The Van Reed's were substantial people, originally from Pennsylvania. James was a retired gold broker and real estate enterpreneur, and their elder son, Eugene, was the

Consul General to Japan, representing the Hawaiian Islands. The house which actually belonged to Julia Van Reed was probably their retirement cottage; they were in their sixties when they moved here. The house appears to have then consisted of two large rooms downstairs and two bedrooms upstairs. The room of rough-sawn redwood (at present the library), with its gray and white marble fireplace, was apparently the parlor. This is the room which may date back even earlier, to the 1840's or 1850's.

Clues to the house's earliest history are to be found in county survey records and deeds. In 1852 James Gale Hubbard applied for a school land warrant for 320 acres on this location (there may have already been a small squatter's cottage here then). The warrants were granted by the federal government to the State of California in 1851 for the erection of schools but subsequently distributed by the state as excess land; in 1857 Hubbell assigned the warrant (modified to 304 acres because of the overlapping boundary of Rancho San Antonio) to Hugh P. Gallagher. But in 1861 Leonard S. Clark actually purchased the land warrant from the state, and after changing hands again, it was in the possession of Warner Buck in 1864. Buck did in fact live in this location probably in the one-and-a-half-story house. At the time of the Moody Road right-of-way hearings in January, 1867 and June of 1868, Mr. Buck protested against the road improvements, declaring that he had his property set off in 5-acre parcels with future "road spaces" already allowed for and that Moody's Road (now El Monte Road in this area) cut diagonally across his land.

But the protests did Warner Buck no good; the road was declared a public highway, and Buck was bankrupt. His property was assigned to a Napa County investor and eventually purchased by Henry Fowler and William Hargrave, also of Napa County; in January of 1872 the State of California patented 141 acres to them. Three months later they gave Julia Van Reed 40 acres of this land.

This rather involved recitation of the change of hands holds special interest here for the student of California history. Henry Fowler was a well known pioneer settler who came to California first in 1844. He is credited with building General Vallejo's Lachryma Montis chalet in Sonoma and several early sawmills in the Napa-Sonoma area. Before the Gold Rush, Fowler operated a 4,000-acre ranch in partnership with William Hargrave; it later was sold to Mormon leader Sam Brannan and became the site of Calistoga.

What prompted these Napa Valley pioneers, who had no known connection to the Santa Clara Valley, to purchase this parcel (and several more surrounding it) and why they gave it to Julia Van Reed is a mystery. Perhaps the connection between Fowler and Mrs. Van Reed is an Hawaiian association. Henry Fowler's father, William, went from Napa County to Hawaii in the late 1850's where, according to family records, he built "thirty homes on speculation." Perhaps the Fowlers and Van Reeds met through Eugene Van Reed in Hawaii or through real estate transactions.

But how does that explain the wording of the April 18, 1872 deed for 40-$\frac{3}{4}$ acres from Henry Fowler and William Hargrave to Julia Van Reed "in consideration of friendship, esteem, regard and affection of parties of the first part for the better maintenance and support of Julia Van Reed"? In any case, the house was now in the hands of a woman and it has continued to be occupied by a parade of interesting women from 1872.

Eccentric heiress Sarah Pardee Winchester, the next woman owner, certainly fits the description. But her sister, Isabelle Pardee Merriman for whom she purchased the house, may be an even more interesting and philanthropic person. Mrs. Merriman, known as a "friend of the helpless," devoted her life to "humane work for man and beast." Although she was concerned for the plight of blacks and was active in the NAACP, her special concerns were for abused children, as well as illegitimate children and their welfare.

While her husband, Louis P. Merriman, operated a vineyard on the property, Isabelle Merriman turned the big house and perhaps the two carriage houses into a haven for homeless or abandoned babies.

In 1905, Sarah Winchester sold a parcel of 105 acres adjoining the Merriman Ranch (which she had purchased years earlier) to Oliver A. Hale, a wealthy merchant, banker, and president of Interurban Railway of San Jose. Apparently Mrs. Winchester did not realize that Hale intended to extend his electric railway from Los Gatos past the Merriman Ranch to Palo Alto. When in 1906 surveyors came out to put in stakes for the laying out of the rail line, Isabelle Merriman and Sarah Winchester were reportedly right behind them pulling them out!

By 1907, the Southern Pacific had taken over Hale's electric railway project and the women apparently gave up.

Sarah Winchester sold the last of her Los Altos holdings, including the Merriman Ranch, to University Land Corporation which seems to have been synonymous with Paul Shoup's Altos Land Company. The Merrimans moved to Palo Alto where Isabelle continued her baby haven while her former home became the center of an even more feminine-oriented operation, a school for girls.

A 1909 promotional brochure on Los Altos described the school, which opened August 20, 1908: "The Chandler School at Los Altos is an outdoor school for girls. Most of the school year classwork and study is out of doors. Sleeping porches have been provided . . . . The beautiful grounds cover six acres. The three roomy buildings used for school purposes are heated by steam and lighted by gas. The school farm furnishes its own fruit, vegetables, eggs, butter and milk. References are required. Mrs. Mary M. Chandler, the principal, will send a descriptive circular . . . . "Mary McDonald Chandler had graduated from Stanford in 1903 and taught at Mills College and Seminary until 1908. Knowing that Mills intended to drop its seminary (high school) shortly, she opened her own school in Los Altos, dedicated to wholesome, healthful living. Her enterprise lasted only a few years; by 1912 it was sold and operated as a boys' school for a short time. In the next several years it changed hands many times, eventually being owned by Ann Feeney Wright and later her daughter, Sarah Wright, members of a pioneer Los Altos family from the neighboring Hale Ranch.

As early as 1887 this white frame house was known as Hidden Villa. The shotgun-toting man on the left may have been a guard on the Mountain View to Pescadero stageline that then traversed the ranch.

Hidden Villa Ranch

26870 Moody Road, Los Altos Hills

Nature lovers from all over the Peninsula know Frank and Josephine Duveneck's Hidden Villa Ranch, an idyllic 1,000-acre expanse in the foothills above Los Altos, open to all those who love and respect the land.

The Duvenecks, founders of the Loma Prieta Chapter of the Sierra Club and active environmentalists, purchased the ranch in 1923. The lush headwaters of Adobe Creek run through their land and its stewardship is carefully guarded by the Duvenecks, who have pledged their ranch to longterm open space. They have many intriguing tales to tell about the picturesque cottage and huge old barn across the way near the banks of Adobe Creek.

The white frame house they say was "brought 'round the Horn" in the late 1840's for "the daughter of the Spanish consul." It is possible that the land was occupied in the mid-nineteenth century by an Hispanic family. It lies close to the eastern border of former Mexican soldier Maximo Martinez' El Corte de Madera Rancho and may have been considered part of it before the final Land Commission decision on the precise rancho boundaries in the 1850's.

It seems more likely, however, that the little cottage (originally three rooms) with its high central gable and jigsawed bargeboard was brought around the Horn for Charles Jones, an early

The Duveneck's Hidden Villa cottage has lost its lush vines and wide porch but still has the last touches of its Victorian trim in the bargeboard that outlines its gabled roof.

resident whose name appears on surveys from 1858 to 1864 but who apparently never received a patent from the government for the land.

When lumber operations began in "The Redwoods," as the entire timber area from Woodside south to Saratoga Gap was called, Moody Road was used to haul logs from the saw pits and mills that dotted Skyline ridge. During this period Hidden Villa cottage is reported to have been a halfway-house where lumbermen stopped their wagons overnight on their way to the bay landings.

The story of the cottage being built for the Spanish consul's daughter probably stems from the ranch's later association with the Walkinshaw family. (In 1882 it was purchased by Robert Walkinshaw, Jr., son of a New Almaden mining man with strong Spanish mercantile connections, and whose brother-in-law William Barron, was the Mexican consul in 1850). Walkinshaw apparently continued using the place as a stopover for a stagecoach operation that had been begun years earlier by George Washington Moody, for whom the road was named.

Moody was with a group of 15 families who came overland to California from Missouri in 1847. Within a short time the young man was married to Emily Lynn, whose family had traveled in the same party. In November of 1849 Washington Moody and his father-in-law James Lynn took over George Harlan's Fremont House near Mountain View, reported to be the first of California's country inns. The Moodys and Lynns continued to own the Fremont House well into the 1860's when Moody went south for a while to the San Joaquin Valley and engaged in cattle trading. Shortly after the start of the San Francisco-San Jose Railroad in 1864, he returned and became interested in the Hidden Villa Ranch area. Much of the surrounding land had fallen into the hands of Charles McLaughlin, who was deeply involved in stage lines and railroads throughout California. There is evidence that the Western Pacific Railroad, which McLaughlin owned, had plans to eventually extend their San Francisco-San Jose Railroad (now part of the Southern Pacific route) westward across the mountains to the coast by way of the El Monte-Moody Road route.

Washington Moody may have heard such rumors. In any case, in April of 1865 he purchased 240 acres on which the cottage stands. His partner in the venture was Simeon Haines, a stage driver and owner of the Bay View House Saloon at the Mountain View Railroad Station. Moody was back in the wayside-inn business. Haines may have attempted to run a stage line at this early date, but it seems more likely that the two men waited until July 1868, when after several unsuccessful petitions Moody's six-mile road was officially declared a public highway. The road was constructed from Haines' Bay View House at the Mountain View Station along part of the old roadway (most of this section is now called El Monte Road) past Moody's house and terminated at the "Mayfield and Pescadero Road" (today's Page Mill Road, which had opened in 1866). By making use of Page Mill Road, which originally included part of Alpine Road, a stage coach could have traveled with relative ease all the way from Mountain View to Pescadero, which by then had been developed as a resort. The Alta California correspondent "Sigma" raved over C. W. Swanton's Pescadero House, and the nearby pebble beach, in his newspaper column of May 19, 1867. The now virtually unknown stage route to Pescadero was apparently used off and on for years.

Indeed when the Duvenecks purchased the ranch in 1923 the cottage still had the trappings of an inn. The original 'round the Horn three rooms had

long ago been expanded to seven. The entire structure was surrounded by a porch and off this a door led into each of the rooms. Across the road—which is an abandoned portion of the original Moody Road—stands a huge old stock barn and blacksmith shop, walls lined with smithy tools from George Washington Moody's era.

The Duvenecks have found many of the tales about Hidden Villa were more fiction than fact. One true story concerned the family of Otto Arnold, who had bought Hidden Villa in 1887 and signed it over in 1903 to his soon-to-be-widowed wife, Katherine. She in turn sold it and moved nearby to an adjacent 27 acres. The eccentric widow became a neighborhood legend, reportedly a "witch." In 1907 she was found dead lying in the dust near the summit of Alpine Road. The wagon that she had been driving had overturned on her. There was talk of foul play to the unfortunate old lady, who was said to have cast evil spells on potential Hidden Villa buyers.

Although the Duvenecks have never felt the effects of Widow Arnold's incantations, they have found evidence of other episodes in Hidden Villa's history. The century-old olive trees said to have been planted by the mission fathers still line the long roadway. Walking through the old barn, the Duvenecks are reminded of the runaway bride who years ago hid there waiting for the stage coach to carry her to her lover in Pescadero.

The Paul Shoup house is an excellent example of craftsman shingle construction.

Supplement

Los Altos ■ Los Altos Hills

Los Altos

Side by side on University Avenue stand the homes of the Shoup brothers, Southern Pacific executives and early developers of Los Altos, who brought the Peninsular Railway through Los Altos in 1907. The brown shingle at **500 University** was built in 1906 by Paul Shoup, who was also a co-founder of *Sunset* magazine, then a travel pamphlet for the railroad. Nearby at **452 University** is brother Guy Shoup's handsome 1912 stucco home.

The Shoup Building at **300 Main Street** has changed little since 1909, when the first school classes and first church services for the Methodist congregation were held in the upper story. The ground floor housed a grocery store. Adjacent at **316 Main** is the old Eschenbruecher Hardware (1909), the town's first commercial structure.

Also downtown on **First Street** is the Mission style Station House of the Peninsular Railroad and Interurban Electric Railway lines, in use from 1913 to 1959. It served as a restaurant from 1962 until 1975. On **San Antonio at Edith**, the J. G. Smith house, built in 1901, will become Los Altos' historical museum.

Other notable pioneer residences may be seen on **University** and **Orange Avenues** and the streets around **San Antonio Road and Main Street.**

The diminutive, steep-roofed Foothill Congregational Church at 461 Orange Avenue, was created by architect Ernest Coxhead in 1917. Additions were made later.

Los Altos Hills

Winding roads that trace the hills yield glimpses of fascinating homes and estates from many eras of development. The 1902 Purissima School on **Duval Way**, visible from Highway 280, is now an Episcopal Chapel. Many barns and tank houses still dot the landscape, but the most noteworthy and easily viewed are structures on **Purissima Road at Roble Ladera**.

Japanese shrine on Foothill College campus.

Conversion of the 1914 Percy Morgan English manor to a private school in 1955 has preserved it well, a good example of how adaptive use can save old mansions from destruction.

Located on the Foothill College campus off El Monte Avenue are the gracious home (1901) of shipbuilder, Willard Griffin, and his former carriage house, now used as a fire station. Also on campus is the fine Henry F. Dana home (1904), now serving as the Faculty Club.

"As the bay recedes . . . around Alviso, now opposite, are numerous gardens from which twenty tons of berries have been shipped in a single day."

The Pacific Tourist *1884*

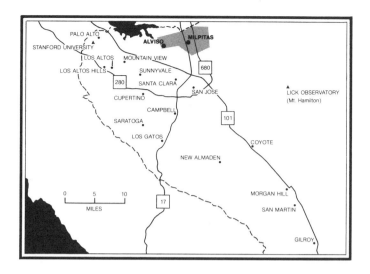

Alviso ❈ Milpitas

There's something special about Alviso. A remote waterfront mystique hangs over the tiny town as thick as the bay fog that engulfs its unpaved streets.

Along the old South Pacific Coast Railroad tracks a derelict store, its windows shot out, sits paradoxically alongside a spanking, freshly painted Victorian. Across the street, the Marina Cafe and bar collects as mixed a bag of characters as you'd hope to find in any old bay port town—boatmen, bait fishermen, unemployed fruit pickers, day sailors, history buffs, businessmen escaping their air-conditioned capsules.

A freelance photographer hangs around snapping snatches of the otherworld quality that pervades Alviso. The streets are nearly always empty and it is quiet—remarkably quiet. Alviso was once the busiest port on the south end of San Francisco Bay, the main link between northern and southern California in the 1850's. Early traders in mission days knew it as the Embarca-dero de Santa Clara where beaver skins, tallow, and hides were ferried by Santa Clara Mission Indians in launches to ships at anchor in San Francisco harbor.

Today its old wharves lie rotting, its ghost-town warehouses sit empty along the once bustling Steamboat Slough. However, a recently completed county marina for pleasure boats hints at pos-·sible rebirth for the little hamlet—the earliest incorporated town in California (1849).

The town survives but its historic name has disappeared from the maps after a continuing battle for identity with its sprawling neighbor San Jose. For years Alviso lay forgotten amid the bay marshes. Then, in the 1960's promoters who had long dreamed of a Port of San Jose, along with others who saw the vast expanse of undeveloped land ideal for an enlarged airport, pushed for

Artist Henry Miller sketched this view of Alviso from "Steamboat Slough" in 1849.

the annexation of Alviso. An election was held in Alviso in January of 1968 and the tiny town's residents apparently approved consolidation; the vote was 189 to 180. The election was challenged, however, by several Alviso townspeople who claimed that non-residents had been lured by the City of San Jose to vote favorably on the question. The County Superior Court ultimately decided in favor of San Jose—the consolidation stands.

The first Mexicans had settled at Alviso in mission days. In the 1840's Ignacio Alviso, the majordomo at the Santa Clara Mission, established his rancho there, near the old Embarcadero.

Shortly after the Gold Rush, four enterprising Yankees dreamed of a city at the southern tip of the Bay. In 1849 they bought parcels of Don Ignacio Al-

viso's Rancho Rincon de los Esteros and the neighboring Barcelia Bernal-Martin's Embarcadero Rancho. They called the place Alviso, for Don Ignacio.

In spite of the sizeable price of $600 per lot, several docks and warehouses were put up along the Guadalupe River for the substantial schooner trade. By 1852 the passenger steamer *Boston*, fare $35 each way, plied the Bay regularly from San Francisco up newly discovered Steamboat Slough to Alviso. Hall and Crandall's Stage connected at the dock, and for an additional $5 would carry travelers over "awful roads" to San Jose. Scores of people came to and through Alviso. California's first American governor, Peter Burnett, lived here; A. P. Giannini's father once farmed 40 acres along the San Jose-Alviso Road.

The advent in 1864 of the San Francisco-to-San Jose Railroad which bypassed Alviso sounded the town's death knell. The decline was slow but sure. In 1876 the South Pacific Coast Railroad passed Alviso's door but the disgruntled seamen and warehouse owners refused for years to allow a station to be erected—blaming the railroads for bursting their burgeoning bubble.

In the 1890's a scheme to restore Alviso to its former glory boomed and busted—a great city, New Chicago, was envisioned rising in the vast plain north of the city. But the area was too far off the mainline of the railway and the project never got off the drawing board.

In 1906 a bright, ambitious Chinese named Tom Foon purchased the struggling Alviso Farmer's Cannery and established the Bayside Cannery —later to become the third largest canning operation in the country. This not only brought new life to the town but greatly changed its character. By 1915, of the nine businesses in town other than the cannery, five were saloons. The Chinese laborers were housed in dormitories at "Chinese Camp" just down the block from the Tilden's house and store.

The National Park Service has taken steps to assure that the Port of Alviso has a place in history by accepting it for inclusion in the prestigious National Register of Historic Places. The register chronicles sites, structures, and districts that have historic integrity, and affords protection from abrupt governmental action. Meanwhile, Alviso lives on in spite of the floods, political turmoil, and loss of its name to San Jose—remarkably absorbing the half dozen factions embroiled in its future.

Just east of Alviso, the town of Milpitas bears little resemblance to the original spot the Spaniards called Penitencia, lying halfway between Mission Santa Clara and Mission San Jose. In early days the neighboring padres met to hear confessions from their parishioners at an ancient adobe confessional near the intersection of the old Oakland-Milpitas Road and Trimble Road. Trimble marks the path to the Mission *milpas*, or corn fields, from which Rancho Milpitas, and later the little town, took its name.

Two Californios lay claim to Rancho Milpitas—Nicolas Berryessa (member of the same family as Rancho San Vicente Berreyesa despite different spelling) and Jose Maria Alviso, both sons of Anza colonists and former soldiers in the San Francisco Presidio Company. Berryessa lost out on his claim because of lack of archival evidence, but Alviso's 4,800-acre grant was confirmed by the U. S. Land Commission in 1853. In the northwest corner of the rancho a village began to emerge along the "Tule Cutoff" from San Jose to the gold fields.

Early in 1856 Frederick Creighton put up a store and established the Milpitas post office. The assistant postmaster was Joseph R. Weller who had previously organized the Milpitas School District and became the local judge and one of the area's most prominent citizens. He took credit for suggesting the name Milpitas for the town—apparently the Yankee settlers were having trouble (as usual) pronouncing the more musical Penitencia.

Although Milpitas' growth has been slow, its citizens have long been noted

Jose Maria Alviso Adobe

Piedmont Road, Milpitas

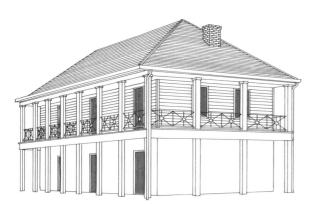

The Jose Maria Alviso adobe, once the center of Rancho Milpitas, as it looked a few years ago.

for their spunk. Back in 1863, when Milpitas was one of the smallest towns in the county, the electrifying Reverend Thomas Starr King held forth at a San Jose political rally. He spotted a sign held high amid the crowd reading "As Milpitas goes, so goes the State." King called attention to the man's self-assurance. The amused crowd quoted the saying and it soon spread throughout the state.

It may have been a prophecy of sorts. After its slow beginnings (an 1895 population of 400, swelling to only 800 by 1922), Milpitas boomed after the advent in 1951 of the Ford Motor plant, growing to 30,000, thereby paralleling the story of California's population boom.

Jose Maria de Jesus Alviso of Rancho Milpitas was the son of Anza colonist Francisco Xavier Alviso, eldest brother of Ignacio Alviso (for whom the town was named). Both were children when they came to San Francisco in 1776. Jose Maria served as a soldier with the San Francisco Company from 1819 to 1827. He had a cousin Jose Maria Alviso, son of Ignacio, with whom he is often confused but who was born in 1812 and would hardly have been old enough to serve in the army in 1819 or to have occupied a rancho in 1830 as did the Rancho Milpitas grantee.*

The fine adobe house that Jose Maria de Jesus Alviso built in the 1830's or early 1840's has a full second story frame addition and veranda, possibly constructed by the original owner before the American occupation rather than after. This may be the "wood two-story adobe" on an extensive prairie a few miles from Mission San Jose reported by Lt. Emmons of Wilkes' Exploration in 1841. Apparently James Alexander Forbes** was living on Rancho Milpitas at that time. (Alviso and Forbes were married to Galindo sisters.) Forbes' house is mentioned in another 1841 journal from the exploration as at "the farm of San Miguel," the name which Jose Maria (de Jesus) Alviso chose to call Rancho Milpitas in contemporary documents.

---

* Documented by Bartolome Sepulveda, great-great-grandson of Jose Maria de Jesus Alviso.

** See Los Gatos, Chapter 7.

Considering its age the house is in a remarkable state of preservation. The ground floor has adobe walls nearly three feet thick now plastered over and painted white; the windows are trimmed with green shutters. Upstairs three large bedrooms overlook the veranda entwined with vintage roses.

At one time there were three other adobes within a thousand yards of the Alviso home place. For years one was used as a winery, and the other two were probably occupied by Alviso's boys Javier and Juan Jose as they established families. Three of Alviso's daughters, Carmen, Augustina, and Maria Antonia, married into the Narvaez family and claimed varying amounts of the 1,145 acres that Jose Maria's widow Juana Galindo de Alviso kept after her husband died in 1853.

In 1855 Alviso's widow married Joseph Urridias from Spain. He acted as guardian of the estate for the three minor children Juan Jose Mario, Maria de Jesus, and Maria de los Angeles. The youngest of the children Maria de los Angeles, and her husband Bartolome Sepulveda later were given 35 acres south of the homestead to farm. Their descendents still hold 15 acres of this land.

In 1871 Juan Maria Alviso's heirs received patent from the United States Government for 4,807 acres. Juana Galindo Urridias, widowed once again, turned over the parcel containing the Alviso adobe to her daughter Carmen. After Juana died in 1882 the remaining rancho property was legally partitioned among the nine heirs. Carmen rented out the 78.89-acre homestead parcel to tenant farmers.

This little girl, a descendent of Jose Maria de Jesus Alviso, is shown in front of one of the four adobes that once stood on Rancho Milpitas. The adobe in this photo was razed in the 1920s.

In 1914 the present owners' family purchased the old home. Sitting in the midst of an old fashioned garden, the adobe was until recently hidden from public view by boards put up by the elderly couple who lived there. They were merely trying to maintain their privacy from the well meaning but disturbing curiosity of old house buffs fascinated to find this bit of Californiana in the hills above Milpitas.

This engraving of a California Ranchero lassoing a steer on the plains near Mission San Jose (in Higuera Country) appears in an 1844 French publication but is thought to be from English artist William Smyth's drawing of 1826, the only California view to appear in the report of Captain F. W. Beechey's British expedition of that year.

The Higuera Adobe and
William Curtner Ranch House

Milpitas

In the mid 1800's the Higueras were the ruling family of the plains and valleys surrounding Mission San Jose. Their haciendas were scattered from Mission San Jose south for several miles into the Santa Clara Valley.

The patriarch Jose Loreto Higuera, son of an Anza colonist, began his career as a *soldado de cuera*, so-called for the distinctive leather jackets which served the Spanish soldiers as an effective armor against Indian arrows. While he was majordomo at Mission San Jose in 1821, Don Jose received Rancho Tularcitos, one of the last ranchos granted while California was still under Spanish rule.

Near the banks of Calero Creek Higuera and his many sons eventually built seven adobe houses. The oldest and largest of them stood for many years topped by a ramshackle frame second story dating from the days when it served as a stage stop hotel. In 1950 the second floor was removed and the original one-story adobe of 1828 was completely reconstructed.

The adobe was originally surrounded by orchards on the north, a vineyard on the east, and vast grain fields on the south. Like most other California rancheros the Higueras did little if any of the planting or cultivating of their agricultural lands. Christianized Indians took care of the farm work as they had done for the padres under the direction of the majordomos.

After Mexico won its independence from Spain and trading ships were allowed into San Francisco Bay, cattle hides became the local currency. Don Jose Higuera's granddaughter, Prudencia, in later years recalled seeing the first American trading vessel off Mission San Jose's Embarcadero in 1839. A horseman from the Peralta Rancho had come to report to the Higueras that a great ship with two masts had entered the bay to buy hides and tallow. The Higueras feverishly rounded up their cattle, bringing them right to the beach, where they slaughtered them and salted the hides. Soon the Yankee captain came to their landing in a small boat; with a sailor as interpreter he invited Prudencia's father, Valentin, to the ship anchored two miles out. The ranchero put on his best clothes, "gay with silver," and went off to the ship while his worried family looked on—afraid they might never see him again.

The next day he returned triumphantly with four boatloads of cloth, axes, shoes, fishing lines, grindstones and jewelry, plus a gun and four toothbrushes. The captain had included a keg of rum which the Higueras reportedly saved only to be used in case of sickness.

Don Jose, nearly 70 in 1845, died in a fall from his horse. So prominent was the family that some of his daughters' husbands took the Higuera name. Each of his twelve heirs received 133 head of cattle, 88 vines, and 10 fruit trees as well as a share in the rancho. Among his heirs was his daughter, Josefa, who had married early California pioneer Robert Livermore and settled a few miles away.

Valentin, the second eldest son, moved with his wife and four children into the large family adobe. Their place became a popular stopping spot on the immigrant trail between Sutter's Fort and San Jose, via Livermore Pass, past Mission San Jose to "Geary's," as the Americans were wont to call Higuera's place. In 1846 during the Mexican War Colonel Francisco Sanchez and his troop of native Californios camped for two days at the Higuera Rancho before engaging in the much debated Battle of Santa Clara.

When pioneer Milpitas landowner Henry Curtner bought the 295-acre Higuera homestead in 1881 the old adobe had been vacant for some time. A few years later Mr. Curtner divided his land holdings among his ten children, and his son William took over the Higuera Ranch. He built a honeymoon cottage there for his bride May, daughter of Milpitas Judge Joseph Weller. The adobe was used as a stable for many years.

The Higuera adobe was completely reconstructed in 1950.

In 1900 William Curtner hired an architect named Binder to build a 14-room, wood-panelled house not far from the adobe on the site of an ancient Indian "sweat house." Curtner's son Weller recalled that his father acted as his own contractor and that a treasure in Indian relics and skeletons were dug up during the laying of the foundation.

After William and May Curtner died, their daughter Marian inherited the property, including the Curtner 14-room ranch house built in 1900, and the Higuera adobe. It was under her supervision that the adobe was reconstructed in 1950 and that a row of 150-year-old olive trees was preserved when construction of Highway 680, which runs along the Curtner-Weller property line, threatened to destroy the heritage trees.

The Wade House and Warehouse

1641 and 1657 El Dorado, Alviso

The Wade prefabricated house lacks any distinctive characteristics of fine architecture, but coupled with its more handsome neighbor, the brick Wade warehouse, it typifies what is most appealing about Alviso—the remote waterfront mystique that pervades the town.

The senior Harry Wade miraculously brought his family through Death Valley the winter of 1849 via the exit route that bears his name. After a successful

The Wade family's four room frame house, prefabricated in New England and shipped around the Horn in the 1850s stands next to H. G. Wade's brick warehouse.

stint at the Mariposa mines, the Wades moved to the Santa Clara Valley where their fifth child Mary Ann was born. In 1851 Harry Wade made the first of dozens of land purchases in Alviso, then a brawny port town.

It is not clear if the extant Wade frame house is the original prefabricated structure that Harry, Sr., bought in 1851 (perhaps relocated due to the constant Alviso floods; it stood, according to the deed, two blocks away at the corner of El Dorado and Taylor Streets) or another one, "brought 'round the Horn in 1855," as reported by his granddaughter, Maggie Wade Higgins, shortly before she died in 1971, aged 94.

Mrs. Higgins was the daughter of Harry George Wade, eldest of Harry

senior's five children. "H. G." as he was called, was 14 when the Wades came to California. He went into the teaming business with his father shortly after they arrived in Alviso. In addition they operated the American House Hotel until it burned down in 1860. He replaced the hotel with the imposing brick warehouse, permanently identified with "H. G. Wade," spelled out in black bricks on one side, which they used for storing the huge volume of hay shipped from Alviso to San Francisco. In 1866 Harry George Wade purchased the warehouse and house property from his father and built wharves on the adjacent land for direct ship-to-shore

The Wade stagecoach was sold to Wells Fargo in 1948.

freighting. Harry senior added stage-coaching to their enterprises and they prospered—in spite of Alviso's declining activity caused by the competition of the San Francisco-San Jose Railroad.

Maggie, the youngest of the junior Wades' family, adored her father. After she graduated from nursing school in San Francisco she returned to Alviso to care for the ailing H.G., a widower confined to a wheelchair. Her brother George still lived at home and continued the family teaming business. A handsome Concord coach was stored in the warehouse in those days, a reminder of H.G.'s unsuccessful attempt to revive the family stagecoach business with a stage line between Alviso and Monterey in the 1870's. In the mid-1880's, another of his ventures, the San Jose and East Oakland Stage Line, lasted only a few months.

When the earthquake hit Alviso in 1906 the Wades may have had some of the Chinese cannery workers (whom they transported back and forth by stage between San Jose and Alviso, 10¢ each way) staying in the top floor of the warehouse. Maggie Wade often told the story of how well the building held, only a few bricks toppling off the upper story as she wheeled her father out of the adjoining house while panicky Orientals ran out of the place. In 1908 Maggie married John Higgins and took her father to spend his final years with them in San Jose, where Higgins was a partner in a mortuary. The house and warehouse were rented out. In 1948 Maggie sold the stagecoach to Wells Fargo's History Room in San Francisco where hundreds see it on display every day.

Susan Ortley Tilden's grandson, Willis Laine, and his family still live in the grand old Victorian house she built in 1887 between the slough and the railroad tracks in Alviso.

The Tilden-Laine House and Store

970 and 996 Elizabeth Street, Alviso

If you have ever been to Alviso you have undoubtedly noted with pleasure if not amazement Susan Ortley Tilden's lovingly cared for Italianate house sitting between the railroad tracks and the slough. It is Alviso's grandest house and the only remaining evidence of the town's good old days.

Built in 1887, the structure is a harmonious blend of Italianate and Eastlake "strip" or "stick" styles, with slanted bay windows and a pillared and bracketed porch curving around two sides. In its early days an iron crested captain's walk topped the hipped roof.

Susan Ortley arrived in California when she was 19 with her just-orphaned half brother and sister. Their mother had died aboard the clipper ship which brought the family from New York around Cape Horn to San Francisco in 1852. Their older brother, John J. Ortley, like his father a seafaring man, ran a line of packets between San Francisco and Alviso, both then booming ports. After her marriage in 1856 to Henry LaBau, Susan and her husband settled in Alviso, as did John Ortley, who married Harry Wade's daughter Almira.

In 1862 the LaBau's paid $90 to the Alviso trustees for title to nearly half of Block 147 on Elizabeth Street. Earlier they had purchased the property from Governor Peter Burnett, one of Alviso's original developers; they built their first house on the site of the existing structure and homesteaded the property in 1865 just a few months before the birth of Susan's second child and the untimely death of Henry LaBau.

Shortly thereafter Susan became Mrs. David Tilden, wife of Alviso's leading merchant and later the town postmaster and justice of the peace. He died in 1875 and the undaunted widow took over his general merchandise store dealing in drugs, liquor, tobacco, boots, shoes, clothing, and hardware, as well as groceries.

With the help of her daughters Marguerite and Minerva the enterprise was apparently successful. They decided to replace the old house with a grander one. In 1887 Alviso had remnants of its earlier affluence. Many substantial houses still lined its streets. Mrs. Tilden's newly built house was even then considered "the finest residence in Alviso, being a large two-story house of modern architectural design."

Susan Tilden died in 1912 and Minerva leased the old store out. She had been married in 1909 to Thomas Ashby Laine, son of one of Santa Clara County's most prominent lawyers, Thomas H. Laine, onetime state senator and member of the Constitutional Convention of 1878.

It was during the 1930's that a clandestine Chinese lottery was rumored held in the Tilden, now Laine, store building. Now, the ramshackle old building has been deserted for years, lying derelict along the railroad tracks —its barred windows shot out—a reminder of the days when Alviso was reported to be a hotbed of gambling, tong wars, and shootings. A Filipino dance hall (charging the usual 10¢ a dance) flourished nearby for a while until it was closed in 1934 after a series of fights and stabbings.

During the following two decades, nothing much except the annual floods took place in Alviso until the annexation battle in the 1960's. Still the Laine family stayed on. Minerva and Tom Laine's son Willis, former Mayor of Alviso, lives with his wife in the beautifully maintained old house; their two sons live a few blocks away.

Supplement

Alviso ■ Milpitas

Early industry in Alviso is marked by the 1858 Old Union warehouse (later part of the cannery next door) at **Hope and Elizabeth**. Next to it stands Yen Chew's Bayside Canning Co., built before 1900 but remodeled in the late 1920's. It is now the Alviso Boat Works. The 1890's false-fronted wooden blacksmith shop on **Liberty** was owned by Wilfred Robidoux, whose house still stands next door on **Taylor**.

The old settlement of Drawbridge exists mostly for duck hunters today. Several shacks remain on **Station Island**, part of Alameda County, and recall the early days before the flooding tides when Drawbridge was a farming community.

Two old ranch houses still exist from the 1860's. Charles E. Wade's two-story frame house, tank tower, windmill, and vine-covered barns are best viewed from **Trimble Road off North First Street**. The William Zanker house on **Zanker Road** between Alviso and Milpitas is a charming two-story Italianate structure.

This turn-of-the-century depot, now a private home, originally sat at Taylor and Eldorado on the west side of the tracks. It was typical of depots built between 1878 and 1904 for the South Pacific Coast Railroad.

The high levee in Alviso now blocks the bay view of the South Bay Yacht Club, whose clubhouse was built about 1905.

"It is embowered in the most luxuriant shrubbery and surrounded with prolific orchards of choicest fruits. It is one of the oldest and most delightfully located towns in the State."

The Pacific Tourist 1884

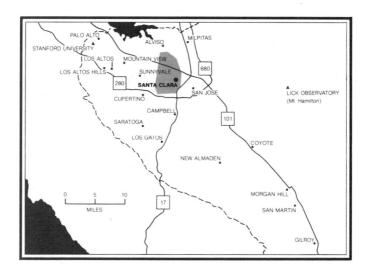

Santa Clara

The Mission of Santa Clara, the town that grew up around it, and the university that bears its name are so closely interwoven that their story is virtually one.

In 1777 California still belonged to Spain. The King's Viceroy in Mexico City had directed that two missions and a military garrison be built on San Francisco Bay to discourage the encroachment from the north by Russian traders. Mission San Francisco had already been established along with the Presidio by October 1776. The following January, Padre Tomas de la Pena, assisted by three Christian Indians brought from Monterey, raised an imposing wooden cross and said Mass under an arbor at the first site of five future churches of Mission Santa Clara. The first and second of these stood near the banks of the Guadalupe River about a mile and a half north of the present location of the University of Santa Clara.

The 1825 mission compound, where the university stands today, was an oasis for rest and refreshment for the frequent travelers along El Camino Real between the ports of Monterey and San Francisco, as well as an important religious community for the Christianization of the native Indians. The *padron* of 1825 showed 1,450 devout souls at Santa Clara, most of whom were Indian neophytes.

In the 1830's "secularization"—the dismantling of the mission system—took place. The original Government decree was enacted in Mexico in 1831, but secularization in California was not actually begun until early in 1834. All temporal powers, property, and lands were taken from the priests' jurisdiction, and a civil commissioner was put in charge at each mission, allegedly to oversee the return of the land to the

69

native population. Secularization was completed at Santa Clara in December 1836 and the land grab began in earnest. In the following chaos hundreds of Indians, victimized and confused, fled. By 1839 there were only 300 Indians left at Mission Santa Clara.

The mission buildings were abandoned by all but the priest and a few loyal neophytes, and the Mexican governor commenced to grant the expansive mission lands almost exclusively to influential Californios, most of whom were officials at the missions or presidios—field foremen, guards, teachers, military escorts, and retired army officers.

This ushered in the celebrated Rancho Days, when the old Spanish ideal of a lord-like Don reigning over vast acres of land became a reality, while the deserted missions fell into decay. Those romantic days, however, were numbered, as slowly, steadily, western expansion of the American frontier approached the Pacific coast, stimulated by the growing port trade with Yankee ships. By 1845 over 300 immigrants had crossed the plains to California. Thousands would soon follow.

The advent of the Mexican War in 1846 marked the beginning of the pueblo of Santa Clara. Many of the settlers sent by Captain Fremont to the mission stayed on at the compound, occupying the abandoned adobe buildings, even setting up a school and holding Protestant Church services there. Some paid rent to the priest in charge—Father Real—others simply "squatted," refusing to vacate the premises. In June of 1847, Military Governor Richard B. Mason found it necessary to send a

troop of U. S. soldiers to remove the squatters and restore possession of the mission to Father Real.

The Gold Rush of 1848 found Santa Clara nearly deserted after gold fever overtook the valley as it did the entire state. With the onslaught of foreigners dozens of Valley Californios fled to the sanctity of the former mission village. By 1850 many new American settlers as well as returning gold hunters arrived in the little pueblo. Early Santa Clara pioneers boasted that it was a spot where the euphonious Spanish language was as often heard as that of the newly arrived Yankees. Padre Real had a town plat of 300-foot-square lots drawn up by surveyor William Campbell and proceeded to sell off parcels of "his" mission lands.

This unholy state of affairs was brought to a sudden halt in 1851. The Catholic Bishop of California saw the need for schools of higher learning in the burgeoning new state. Those experienced educators—the Order of the Society of Jesus, the Jesuits—were asked to come to Santa Clara, replace Padre Real, restore the mission buildings, and establish the College of Santa Clara, the first college in California. That summer 12 eager young men enrolled at what would eventually become the University of Santa Clara.

This action seemed to have a stabilizing effect on the place, and in 1852 an official government of duly elected trustees was established; Santa Clara legally became a town.

This 1840 deed from Governor Alvarado to Jose Pena grants him a house in the Rancheria at Mission Santa Clara.

Gobernors. Alvarado + Pico Pico Tte. José Peña
1839

Expediente promovido por D. José Peña en pretencion de una casa
del Establecimiento de Sta. Clara

9/30+

Sello Quarto una Quartilla
Habilitado provisionalmte. por la Aduana Maritima de Monterey para los
años de 1839 y 1840   Antonio Mª. Pico
Alvarado

Por Prefecto del Primer Distrito
José Peña Teniente de Premio Retirado ante la Superioridad
de V.S. con el debido respeto y derecho que haya lugar, se presenta
y dice: que en el año de mil ochocientos treinta, teoría de alcance de
su sueldo del Premio la cantidad, que espera la copia de Ajuste que
me hize el Sor. D. Manuel Ignacio Casarin, entonces Comisario,
y considerando el que hasta fines del año Beinte y ocho, debo te-
ner una alcance bien considerable, el cual Eccedo al Gobierno, en tal
de que se me de una casa de las de la Pancheria de Sta. Clara, de
la ultima Quadra que miran por la Huerta para de ese modo Ridici me
y acabar mis dias. Por tanto. Suplico tenga abien atender a mi solici-
tud haciendo uso de su bondad de que lo haré reconosido
Sta. Clara 29 de Abre de 1839.
José Peña

Señor Prefecto del 1er. Distrito.
La casa que pretende el espresante no se halla ocupada hace mucho
tiempo, y en concederse ta no se perjudica al Establecimiento, por que
el reducido numero de Indigenas que hay no pueden llenar las que
estan fabricadas: es cuanto puedo informar a V.S. sobre el particular.
Santa Clara 11 de Enero 1840.   José R. Estrada

Sn. Juan de Castro Enero 15 de 1840.
Con el informe de esta Prefectura elevese al Exmo Sor. Gobernador del
Departamento   Castro

Exmo Sr. Gobernador.
Impuesta la Prefectura de la pretencion del teniente de premio Dn.
José Peña del informe que dio el Administrador de Sta. Clara en-
cuentra por adaptable la concesion del edificio ó casa que se pret
Sello Quarto una Quartilla.
Habilitado provisionalmte. por la Aduana Maritima de Monterey para los
Alvarado   años de 1839 y 1840   Antonio Mª. Pico

tunde, fundado en que el Establecimiento dicho no lo necesita, y en
que el interesado debiendo á la Nacion una suma que le es debida
por sus haberes, tendrá en la avanzada edad en que se halla una
habitacion en que vivir, y la satisfaccion de ser recompensados en
parte por el Gobierno, sus servicios en la carrera militar.
Sn. Juan de Castro enero 15 de
1840.
José Castro

The Pena Adobe*

3260 The Alameda, Santa Clara

The earth-colored adobe sits far back from the street amid pines and olive trees. It is dark and cool under the wooden portico protecting the ancient mud brick walls. For longer than anyone can remember it has stood there near the old Mission Road. The dwelling's origin has been studied and debated for years, which is not surprising, for it has had many lives.

This is the sole survivor of the third mission compound (dedicated in 1784), and it was probably standing in 1792 when English explorer Vancouver came to Santa Clara. His record of the visit noted that, directed by the fathers, a number of the more industrious Indians were "building for themselves a range of small, but comparatively speaking comfortable and convenient habitations—each consisting of two commodious rooms below with garrets over them."

Thirty such "apartments" for young married Indian couples were built of mud bricks and roofed with tiles by 1798. Five parallel rows of these dwellings ran westerly from the Murquía Church and made up what University Archivist Arthur D. Spearman, S. J. refers to as the Rancheria d'esta Mission. The padres also called the native Indian villages of tule huts "Rancherías," but there is no doubt this adobe belonged to Mission Santa Clara's Ran-

chería. After months of searching, the deed granting the house to Jose Pena was located in a dusty old book of patents in the county courthouse basement. It reads in part "una casa de las de la Ranchería de Santa Clara" ("a house of those of the Ranchería of Santa Clara").

The gentleman referred to is Don Jose Pena, grantee of Rincon de San Francisquito. He was one of the most ambitious, intelligent men of California's Mexican period. Fully aware of the value of land, he petitioned for seven land grants. Though he took possession of only two of these, he left his unique mark up and down Alta California. As lieutenant of artillery, elector, teacher, commissary, and acting administrator, he served at San Diego, Monterey, San Francisco, and his last years at Santa Clara.

In his will, Don Jose, who died in 1852, describes his house as of eight rooms. Evidently he had acquired four of the neophyte apartments in lieu of back salary when Governor Alvarado granted him the casa and 100 varas of surrounding land in 1840. His salary complaints are recorded in correspondence to the civil authorities. It seems Pena was not only a teacher of Santa Clara's "Book School"—forerunner of the college—but after secularization kept the account books and was in charge of the storehouses—a heavy schedule for a man in his sixties.

Santa Clara was swarming with Americans in the 1850's, and Pena's widow Gertrudis and her widowed daughter-in-law Concepcion found their property in demand. They began

* State Registered Landmark #249

selling off parcels of their 300-foot-square block, holding on to the area immediately surrounding the adobe house. Dona Gertrudis even resold Rincon de San Francisquito to a willing gringo buyer in 1859. Concepcion's sister Magdelena Guerrero married former Kentuckian Henry Brother, 13 years her junior, who had bought an adjoining lot.

The Guerrero sisters must have carried their years well. In 1858 Magdelena gave birth to a son—she was 44 years old. Concepcion, who was two years older, began keeping company with the deputy county recorder, Henry Uhrbrook, 14 years younger than she. He had also bought property in the Pena's Block 51 and when Maria Refugia, the Indian girl who was raised by the Pena's, married John Bassford, another landowner in the block, the neighborhood was literally one big family. They delighted in attending the bull and bear fights just two blocks away at the public plaza on the Alameda.

After Jose's widow died, Concepcion rented part of the adobe, keeping the two northern rooms and a lean-to kitchen as her residence. Mattie (Magdelena), Henry, and family lived with her for a few years. The little place seems hardly large enough for so many, but the Mexican-Californians rarely built their adobes larger than the few rooms they needed. One room, often with a raised fireplace, served as a dining room and master bedroom while the other room was used for childrens' sleeping, sewing, and general work. The kitchen was usually separated from the house.

A tile floored veranda now fronts the Pena adobe protected by a substantial tile roofed overhang.

A hard earthen floor was typical in an adobe no matter how lordly or grand the owner or rancho might be. Each room had a door opening on a corridor or covered veranda along the front, and usually one small window cut into the three-foot thick adobe walls.

The Pena adobe in the 1880s; one of the two women may have been Concepcion Pena who lived here until her death in 1883. Only the extant two northern rooms remained intact at this date; heavy damage from the torrential rains of 1861–62 may have destroyed the adjoining adobe apartments.

In March of 1883 Concepcion died, leaving everything to her "only sister" Magdelena Brother—personal property of $12 and real estate valued at $600, consisting of Lot 7 and dwelling house thereon (yearly rental $60) and Lot 2, same block, and dwelling thereon. The latter is the surviving adobe house.

The Daroche family rented the house for many years thereafter from Mattie. She and Henry had their own house on the adjacent corner by that time. After the untimely death of her daughter in 1888 she became very close to the four Daroche girls.

Doughty old Mattie had outlived nearly everyone when she died in 1902. Bent with age (she was barely over four feet tall), contemporary news items referred to her as "the oldest resident of Santa Clara—believed to be over 100 years old" (actually she was 88).

Her only surviving relative, Thomas Brother, came into possession of the adobe. There is no evidence that he lived in the house more than one year; only in 1905 is he listed there in the local directory. Thomas liked to tell how during the 1906 quake he stood in the doorway of the adobe and watched all the other buildings in town "tumble down." He loved the Pena adobe and took special care of it up to 1911, when the 92-year-old bachelor died.

The Santa Clara Women's Club had their eye on the place. (They believed the adobe had been a mission dormitory for Indian women at one time.) When it was sold as part of Thomas Brother's large estate they raised $350 and purchased the house and the 60 by 147-foot parcel surrounding it. On June 24, 1914 at an impressive civic ceremony the adobe, now the headquarters of the Women's Club, opened amid much fanfare. The women had spent $400 remodeling the venerable structure, laying a wooden floor over the ancient earthen one and repairing the original tile roof. A small dormer opening in the original roof was removed. Since then a fine carved wooden door and Spanish tile floor have been added as well as a large modern recreation room in the rear. But the old adobe walls, cracks and all, still stand as they did when Don Jose Pena lived here in the oldest house in Santa Clara County, if not the oldest in California.

Mission Santa Clara's original adobe tower was already enclosed in wood when this early 1850s photograph was taken. The entire 1822–25 church was destroyed by a fire in October of 1926; the present church is a replica of the original.

Mission Santa Clara*

On grounds of the University of Santa Clara, The Alameda

When the earthquake of 1822 hit, the priests at Mission Santa Clara were already prepared to dismantle the third of the Mission churches, Padre Jose Murguia's remarkably beautiful building of 1784. It had been severely damaged by prior quakes in 1812 and 1818 and the priests had undertaken the building of a new, but temporary, chapel just over a thousand yards southward. Later this became the Indian boys' dormitory. From here the saintly Padre Magin Catala guarded the altar and along with Padre Jose Viader supervised the construction of the permanent church and final Mission Santa Clara compound, begun in 1822 and completed with the dedication of the church on August 11,

1825, the eve of St. Clare's feastday. (Mission Santa Clara, appropriately named for Santa Clara de Asis who in 1212 founded the Second Order of St Francis, was "sister" mission to that of Mission San Francisco de Asis, named for the founder of the order of Franciscan Friars to which Father Serra and all the Alta California mission padres belonged.)

Ignacio Alviso,** who after secularization was majordomo at the mission, took credit for serving as construction foreman of the entire 1822–25 compound. The 200-foot quadrangle within the compound was made up of the church, storerooms, priests' residence, and quarters for young Indian neophyte

---

* State Registered Landmark #338

** See Chapter 4, Alviso.

The old "adobe wall" is actually all that remains of the south wing of the mission quadrangle which housed the Indian girls' spinning wheels and looms.

struction took place during the years just following the Mexican War of Independence from Spain when the new Mexican government had taken possession of the Jesuit Pious Fund of the Californias which had previously been a major source of support for the missions.

It is often reported that *nothing* remains today from the 1822–25 compound; but a few remnants are extant, in spite of the years, progress (which usually is characterized by the obliteration of our heritage), and a disastrous fire in October 1926 that destroyed the mission church.

South of the mission gardens (where only a few olive trees remain from mission days) is the old adobe wall, actually not part of the outer mission walls (which were washed away by torrential rains in 1861–62) as is often assumed. It was the north wall of the south quadrangle wing (16' by 200'), housing the spinning wheels and looms where the Indian girls learned and practiced the craft of blanket weaving and dressmaking.

West of this wall and also dating from 1822 is the Adobe Lodge which made up the west wing of the quadrangle. Unfortunately greatly remodeled, today it is the Faculty Club for the University of Santa Clara. It originally was the granary storehouse, and is of special interest as the first quarters of Father John Nobili, the Jesuit priest who took charge of the decaying mission in March of 1851 and two months later opened the College of Santa Clara, California's first institution of higher education which achieved university status in 1855.

girls. Outside the quadrangle were guardhouse, jail, and six houses for guards; the buildings were of adobe and had tiled roofs. The mission establishment was completed in less than four years—a feat reported to be accomplished at no other mission. This was especially remarkable since the con-

Fernando Berreyesa brought his wife, Catarina, to this adobe in Santa Clara in 1862 to escape the battles over his father's rancho at New Almaden.

Fernando Berreyesa's Adobe

373 Jefferson Street, Santa Clara

On the edge of the original town of Santa Clara a modest little house, gaily trimmed in brilliant orange, sits in the shade of a huge gnarled olive tree. The story of Fernando Berreyesa, the owner of this old adobe involves one of the most fascinating sagas of early California, that of the Berreyesas of New Almaden and the desperate battle for their land.*

When in August 1861 Maria Zacarias Bernal de Berreyesa bought this parcel of former Mission Santa Clara land from the Galindo family, the adobe house was already there. Experts have guessed it dates from the late 1840's because of the size of the adobe brick, 18 by 12 inches. (Most bricks made under the direction of the padres were 22 by 11 inches.) However, according to

---

* See Chapter 8, New Almaden.

local lore the building was once a mission jail for unruly Indian field hands. And since it has an outside staircase leading to an upstairs garret, not unlike Vancouver's description of the Indian "apartments" of 1792*, the structure may in fact have been constructed earlier than is generally supposed. A charming attempt at homemade carved wood trim adorns the veranda along the front of the house. In the rear a frame addition of two rooms has been added to the original three adobe rooms.

The widow Berreyesa gave the property to her son Fernando, who brought his wife Catarina and their many children here to live after selling their interest in the Berreyesa Rancho near the famous New Almaden Mine. A contemporary described the family: "The Bernals, and the Berreyesas (of whom Don Jose Santos was particularly noble looking and intelligent) were all fine looking, proud and dignified in address and manners, the cream of the country." Fernando's wife Catarina was a member of the Castro clan.

Fernando's father, Jose Reyes Berreyesa, had been a soldier at San Francisco Presidio where his father, Nicolas, came as a boy with Anza's party of settlers to found San Francisco in 1776. In 1834 the Berreyesas settled 10 miles south of Pueblo San Jose on Rancho San Vicente. In 1842 Reyes petitioned Governor Alvarado for the rancho, "two sites in the Canada de Los Capitancillos," noting that he had served in the army for 24 years, for which he received no pay, and that he had 11 children. He complained that his neighbor Justos Larios "disturbed my repose," little anticipating that the successors to Larios'

nearby Rancho Capitancillos and a variety of adventurers would more than disturb the lives of his family in the stormy years ahead.

In 1845 the Mexican government sent Captain Andres Castillero to California in search of mineral deposits. At Mission Santa Clara, Padre Real and his cousin, Majordomo Secundino Robles,** told him about an old abandoned mine in the hills near the Berreyesa Rancho. Samples were taken which Castillero realized were rich in quicksilver deposits and a partnership was formed between Padre Real, the Robles brothers, Castillero, and Jose Castro (then commanding general of California's tiny army). They had unaccountably excluded Jose Reyes Berreyesa, on whose land they knew the mine lay. In protest, on January 2, 1846, Reyes served public notice of having discovered what he thought was a "copper vein" on his rancho and applied for a mining grant. In June of 1846 Reyes' son, Jose de los Santos, who was first alcalde (mayor) of Sonoma, was taken prisoner by the Bear Flag insurgents and put in prison with two of his younger brothers. Their distraught mother, Maria Zacarias, insisted that Reyes go to Sonoma to check on their condition. The "pacific old man," then 61 years old, left Santa Clara for San Pablo where he was taken by boat along with the de Haro twins, cousins of his wife, to a landing near San Rafael. As they headed toward the mission they

---

* See the Pena Adobe, this chapter.

** See Chapter 1, Palo Alto—Mayfield—Stanford.

were confronted by none other than Kit Carson and two other men under Captain Fremont's command who deliberately shot them down, stripped their bodies and left them lying there. It was just the first of a staggering series of tragedies to strike the Berreyesas.

The significance of a rich cache of quicksilver in California increased tremendously with the discovery of gold in 1848; the mine and Rancho San Vicente became the hottest piece of real estate around. The history of the mine and the litigation involved is too voluminous to summarize here. It started in 1850 when the Berreyesa's attempted to eject the mine developers for trespassing on their land and continued for 14 years until the final settlement in 1864. But little has been said of the tragic consequences to the lives and property of Jose de los Reyes Berreyesa and his heirs.

Fernando, one of the youngest of the seven Berreyesa boys, married Maria Vicente (called "Catarina") Rodriguez on August 13, 1849 at Santa Clara Mission Church and took his 15-year-old bride to Rancho San Vicente where each of the brothers had his own house. The Berreyesa boys were known to jealously protect their property from intruders while they were attempting to gain confirmation from the U. S. Land Commission. In July 1854 the bullet-ridden body of a man who had lived near the Berreyesa's rancho was found in a gully on their land. In retaliation, a band of armed and masked men burst into the home of Encarnacion, the youngest Berreyesa son, dragged him off and hanged him, leaving him for dead. The bloodthirsty gang then forced their

Catarina Rodriguez Berreyesa in 1936 at the age of 102.

way into his brother Nemesio's home and took him to San Jose, where he was found the following day hanging dead from a tree. (A coroner's inquest held shortly thereafter found no evidence that either young man was responsible for the killing on their property, noting however that this particular family was regarded as "violent, brutal, revengeful and bloodthirsty.") Encarnacion had not died and luckily was found and cut down in time to save his life, but the incident left him understandably deranged. He signed his rights to San Vicente over to his brothers and retreated to Santa Barbara. But in 1857 the tormented fellow was killed by *another* lynch mob in the aftermath of a search for a band of Mexican outlaws.

Another series of unbelievable events seemed foredoomed to plague the lives of three other sons of Jose Reyes. Santiago Berreyesa, eldest of the brothers, was apparently deeply disturbed by the elopment of his 14-year-old niece with a young man from Chile. On November 18, 1855 he went to the house of his brother Ygnacio, where the couple lived, and aiming through the window shot and killed the young husband as he sat beside his bride. Santiago fled immediately to Mexico and vanished without a trace. A year later at Francisco Berreyesa's house near the New Almaden mines, the strangest of all the disasters took place when a man who had been visiting the Berreyesa's said goodnight and pretended to leave the house, but actually hid himself under

the bed! Francisco's wife discovered him and when Berreyesa pulled the man out by the hair, he pulled a knife, stabbed Berreyesa, and escaped into the night. Francisco died the next day. (The strange circumstances recorded in a reliable county history have never been explained further.)

Meanwhile the Berreyesa's claim to Rancho San Vicente ground its way through the courts. At last in 1860 the U. S. Supreme Court confirmed their title to the grant. With incontestable relief the Berreyesa heirs sold all rights and title to the mine developers for $42,500 (a tiny fraction of the eventual millions New Almaden Mine earned for its shareholders). There were only two surviving Berreyesa brothers in California—Jose Santos, who lived on his wife's rancho in Contra Costa County, and Fernando, still living on the Rancho San Vicente. The following year Fernando and family moved to the adobe in Santa Clara.

A few years after Dona Maria Zacarias died in 1869, Catarina convinced Fernando to leave the Santa Clara Valley where they had known so much sadness and move to Watsonville where her family had its roots. Catarina had been born in the little pueblo of Branciforte (now part of Santa Cruz) where her father Francisco Rodrigues had been alcalde in 1830. He had long since sold his Rancho Los Coyotes, but her brothers and sisters were heirs to her grandfather Joaquin Castro's Rancho San Andres west of Watsonville, and still lived in the area. In 1873 the Berreyesas moved nearby to the village of Santa Rita (also called for a short time "New Republic") on the San Juan Bautista Road.

About this time the ominous litany of violence that had pursued the family caught up even with them. One afternoon Fernando was at the New Republic Race Track when he engaged in a vehement argument over the results of one of the races. The proud Fernando may have suggested the duel which followed. Reports vary—either Fernando's bullet hit its mark, but his opponent Charles Robertson's pocketed keys deflected the bullet and he fired at Fernando, or Robertson took only eleven of the required thirteen paces before turning and firing. Either way, Fernando, the last of the New Almaden Berreyesas, was shot and died that day at Santa Rita. That the tale is hazy on details is understandable. In 1935 Catarina Berreyesa, then 101 years old, told one version of the event and said that it took place in 1882. In 1937, having just celebrated her 103rd birthday, Catarina was interviewed and related the second version of the tragic story as happening in 1875. She was still living at Santa Rita with her youngest son Fernando and his wife (who reported that the spry old lady still cooked her own dinner, in the Mexican style). Just a few weeks before she reached her 104th birthday Catarina Rodriques Berreyesa died. She had outlived all but one of her twelve children. She was buried at the cemetery at Santa Rita not far from where Fernando died many years before.

Judge Hiram G. Bond at his ranch, New Park, in 1900.

New Park

Lincoln Street, Santa Clara

In *Call of the Wild* Jack London describes "a big house in the sun-kissed Santa Clara Valley . . . half hidden among the trees." London's immortal dog, Buck, lived there amid the rows of vine-covered servants' cottages, the stables, lush grape arbors, orchards, and berry patches.

The ranch which so impressed London was New Park—so named in 1866 by mining and lumber tycoon James P. Pierce for his grandfather's country home in England. Originally developed as a 95-acre estate by financier William Lent in 1856, ten acres of New Park survive today as the cloister for a community of Carmelite nuns who live in total seclusion walking to prayer from their rooms in the former carriage house, passing beneath the old grape arbor, five carriage-widths across.

Before the turn of the century Jack London would come down on the train to Santa Clara to visit his fellow gold hunters from Klondike days, Marshall and Louis Bond. Their father, Judge Hiram Bond, a self-made millionaire, had bought New Park from the Pierce family in 1895. The estate, with its tennis courts, summer houses, winery, and acres of orchard, was just what the dynamic former Wall Street financier was looking for when he expanded his mining interests to the West Coast.

The large, modified Georgian house (razed in 1916 to make way for the Carmelite chapel) was filled with the judge's antiques and historical books collected through the years. His enterprises had carried him from Harvard Law School to a federal judgeship in Virginia, back to New York, and finally to mining interests in Colorado, New Mexico, the Northwest, and San Francisco.

In the gold fields around the Klondike the judge's sons met Jack London among the other young gold hunters in 1897. They spent the winter together, hoping to find a rich strike. London returned to Oakland that spring, sick with scurvy. Marshall and Louis, apparently unsuccessful in their quest, went home

to Santa Clara in June of 1898. They both married and settled down at New Park for a few years.

Jack London was a frequent visitor to the Bond Ranch during those years. Local pub owners near the railroad stop recalled his visits while he waited to be picked up by the Bonds. There is local speculation that the canine hero of London's famous novel, *Call of the Wild*, was one of a pair of dogs that the Bond brothers had taken with them to the Yukon. Prototype of London's Buck, the Bond's dog, Jack, was presumably brought back to New Park when the brothers returned home. Santa Clara oldtimers swear it was Buck himself that they saw, trotting back and forth from New Park to the market with a basket slung around his neck.

In 1905 Judge Bond lost the Midas touch. All of his enterprises suddenly went sour. He put New Park on the market and with his wife Laura moved to Seattle, where he died of a heart attack two months later.

By then Louis was off in the Nevada gold fields. Marshall had resumed his search for adventure. In 1902 he took part in a wild scheme to colonize Mexico by importing Boers from the Transvaal. Off to the Nevada gold fields he went in 1904. Later he wandered from one exotic spot to another—big game hunting in Canada, silver mining in Mexico, on safari in the Belgian Congo—finally settling down in Santa Barbara at the age of 65.

The chapel of the Carmelite nuns was designed by architects McGinnis and Walsh of Boston who modeled its bell tower after one in Avila Spain where St. Theresa the founder of the Carmelites was born.

New Park was rented and used as a private rest home for a time until Senator James Phelan* and his nephew Noel Sullivan purchased the property for the use of the Carmelite nuns in memory of Phelan's sister, Alice Phelan Sullivan. She is buried there in the beautiful Spanish Renaissance Chapel built in 1917 as part of the monastery where her daughter, one of the Carmelite sisters, still lives.

---

* See Villa Montalvo, Chapter 6, Saratoga.

The Arguello house on Santa Clara Street now converted into apartments is little changed in its exterior from its original appearance.

The Arguello House

1085 Santa Clara Street, Santa Clara

I felt sure my research was going to result in some interesting historical discoveries when five years ago I literally happened across this unheralded landmark gem, a house that belonged to the family of Luis Antonio Arguello, California's first governor under Mexico from 1822 to 1825 (and the son of Jose Dario Arguello, governor under Spain from 1814 to 1815). In 1857, Soledad Ortega de Arguello, widow of Governor Luis Arguello, returned to Santa Clara where off and on through the years since her husband's death in 1830 she and her children had lived in

one of the mission buildings. The Arguello claim to Rancho Pulgas (35,000 acres in San Mateo County) had been confirmed and apparently she felt the family could return to the mission town where they had spent so many years.

The widow Arguello paid $1,000 for half a city block fronting 100 yards on Main Street and 50 yards on Santa Clara Street. The land she purchased is noted on the deed as "part of the Mission"; it had been the horse corral with sections set aside for cattle, sheep, and swine, and surrounded by a 10-foot adobe wall until 1852. There already was a house standing on the parcel, built by a Samuel Scott, which is probably incorporated in the rear of the present structure. At first Senora Arguello and her two sons, Jose Ramon and Luis Antonio and their families, all lived in this house, which must have been enlarged to near its contemporary size with the major addition fronting on Santa Clara Street as it does today.

Within a few years Jose Ramon built a fine mansion next door on Santa Clara and Washington Streets for his wife, Ysabel Alviso, and their growing family. His mother Soledad moved in with them and continued to live there until her death in 1874. In her will she bequeathed the first house to her son, Luis Antonio, who had been living there continuously since 1857.

Little is said of Luis Antonio Arguello in historical records. Bancroft merely records he was the son of the first Mexican governor and in 1885 was still a resident of Santa Clara. He was born at San Francisco Presidio in 1830, just four months after his illustrious father died. The Arguellos are often mentioned as the cream of Californio society. They claimed pure Spanish ancestry (important to the caste system of the times) and their education was apparently above average for the outpost of empire that was Alta California. At age 22, Luis married another member of top Californio society, Angela Berreyesa, daughter of Jose Ygnacio Berreyesa of the New Almaden family.*

In 1870, according to that year's census record, the Luis Arguello household consisted of "Louis [sic] Arguello, retired farmer, real property of $30,000 and personal property of $11,500, his wife Angela, and eight children." In 1880, Luis is listed as a "capitalist" and three more children have been born, including the youngest, "Maggie," age

Luis Antonio Arguello and his wife, Angela, circa 1870.

---

* See Berreyesa Adobe, this chapter, and Chapter 9, New Almaden.

two. "Don Luis" as he preferred to be called, has been said by his descendents to have been violently "Anti-anglo." In researching his personal papers I find no evidence of this. The children apparently used Americanized versions of their names and several of them married Americans. Luis was involved in commercial operations with Americans; and after his wife Angela's death, his American "godchild" moved into the big house along with Luis' children James, Luis, Jr., and Maggie.

Two years before Luis died in 1898 he married a woman named Edelfrida, a situation which did not please some of his six surviving children. His will, which did not include the Santa Clara house, was contested but held. Margaret Arguello (Maggie) had been given the old house sometime prior to May 1898 when Don Luis made out his will. In 1901 she sold it to the family of Dr. George Worrall, a leading Santa Clara dentist. He converted part of the house into an office and retained the rest as a residence. After his death in the 1920's his wife conducted a rest home there.

In 1940, Peter J. Pasetta, a local building contractor, bought the Arguello house and remodeled it into seven spacious apartments. Mr. Pasetta admits to extensive rebuilding inside the old place but his statement that the exterior remained nearly intact is borne out by photographs of the earlier structure.

James Lick's Mansion

Montague Road (Agnew vicinity)

James Lick is not generally thought of as a Santa Clara Valley personality. This strange man who left an unparalleled legacy of benefits to his adopted state is usually thought of as a San Franciscan, in spite of his magnificent gift of the Lick Observatory on Mount Hamilton* southeast of San Jose.

However, the mansion he built circa 1858 and a round brick warehouse from his remarkable flour mill of 1855 ("the like of which has never been seen in the world") are living evidence of Lick's strong ties with Santa Clara.

Legend has it that it was the memory of his "lost love," the daughter of a wealthy Pennsylvania mill owner, that prompted this "shabby millionaire" to construct his elaborate near-baronial estate, which cost him well over $300,000. The house as well as the interior of the main mill building (which burned down in 1882) were paneled with imported cedar, mahogany, and native California laurel. James Lick, who was an excellent wood craftsman and piano maker by trade, worked on the installation himself. The two-story house, built between 1858–60, was inaccurately supposed to have been inspired by Mount Vernon. The pillared front veranda and pediment on the roof are slightly reminiscent of plantation houses, but the general aspect of Lick's mansion is distinctly Italianate (as was his Lick House Hotel in San Francisco), here in a less formal variation with

---

* See Chapter 8, San Jose.

After eccentric James Lick's mill was sold his house became the subsequent mill superintendent's residence.

round arches, consoled "blind" pilasters and a true balustrade above the regular pillars of the veranda.

James Lick is said to have built the 24-room, 24-fireplace house so his illegitimate son, John, who at age 37 in 1855 had come from Pennsylvania (as had Lick's nephew James H. Lick), could live with him on the estate. But John, who has been described as slow moving, unambitious, and disobedient, preferred the simple room in a cabin where he had lived before.

One year later Lick also moved out, back to a shanty near the mill where he had previously stayed. He had furnished only a few rooms in the mansion—his own bedroom where he kept his numerous scientific and metaphysical books, and the living room, which was furnished with a table, a few chairs, and a grand piano.

In 1863 John returned to Pennsylvania and shortly thereafter James Lick offered the mill for sale, but the yearly floods that had inundated the mill were too widely feared. No one offered his

asking price of $250,000 (by then the entire operation including flood levees had cost him over $500,000). So in 1873, because he had admired Thomas Paine, he gave the mill to the Thomas Paine Society in Boston, which immediately sold it for a mere $18,000 to Pfister and Waterman, paper manufacturers. Lick never forgave them. Meanwhile, Lick, more cantankerous than ever, had moved to an unpretentious house in south San Jose. The move took more than two years to complete. He transplanted dozens of trees from the magnificent gardens he had put in years earlier at the mill.

But much of the gardens must have remained. For many years, Lick's Mill, as it continued to be called, was a favorite outing spot. Visitors would take the steamer from San Francisco to Alviso and ride a special stageline to the mill to picnic and walk among the grape arbors, golden willows, and cork oaks or feed the swans in the small lake in front of the mansion, which was then the paper mill superintendent's residence. In the late 1890's a group of San Francisco bankers purchased the place and converted "Lick's Folly" into an alcohol distillery operation. For more than 50 years it has been the headquarters for a variety of chemical companies.

James Lick, the enigma, variously described as intelligent, honest and industrious, and again, "avaricious, unwashed and unsocial," died in 1876 and by bequests in his will became one of the greatest of California's benefactors, memorialized in parks, schools, observatories, and a California freeway.

Lick's mansion in Santa Clara near Agnew.

Alviso Street north of Franklin *has two excellent false-fronted structures—the last vestiges of the once powerful German Colony in Santa Clara. Santa Clara Verein, the German-American Lodge Hall and its neighbor across the street, known as the Larder House (top photo), reputed to be a former stage stop, look just as they did when built in the late 1860's or early '70's.*

Supplement

Santa Clara

Santa Clara's original 1850 town plat is marked by square blocks between El Camino Real on the north, The Alameda on the east, south to Bellomy and west to Lincoln. Despite the devastating removal of the old business district, the city maintains its strong historical character with dozens of mid-nineteenth century structures—many well preserved.

Examples from the 1850's, when rustic variants of more fashionable eastern styles were popular, include: **1210 Jefferson at Fremont**, where the old Higgins House has been continuously occupied by the same family; the Johnson House on **Main between Fremont and Benton** was originally shipped in pre-cut sections from New England around Cape Horn and was restored in the 1930's; and the simple well-maintained frame structures at **1075 and 1045 Benton**, between Main and Washington, which served as home and separate office for Dr. Saxe at a time when having an office inside the home was customary.

The 1866 Jamison House was extensively remodeled in the 1930's and has been relocated at Triton Museum **in the Civic Center**. The quoins that define and appear to reinforce the corners of the once two-story frame house define parts of the original structure.

At **Fremont and Main** is the 1865 home of Cary Peebels, who was identified in the 1876 directory as a ''farmer and capitalist''—typical occupational description of the late century.

Southern Pacific's railroad depot, located at the **foot of Franklin**, has been in use continuously since 1868.

A favorite of Santa Clarans, this simplified Victorian Gothic house at 1217 Santa Clara Street was owned and built by Andrew Landrum in 1875.

Other 1870's structures worth noting are three well-maintained two story frame houses. The house at 1889 Market was built by Albert Harris, a town trustee and vice president of the Santa Clara Valley Bank, and later owned by Captain Frederick Lass, a retired sea captain. The J.J. Miller house at 1206 Main is marked by decorative quoins, or corner supports. The house that pioneer Calvin Russell built in 1873 at 1184 Washington was later owned by John Robinson, one of Santa Clara's first druggists, and until 1942 the house was not wired for electricity.

Two charming board-and-batten frame houses with unusual roofs and fine carpentry details on Madison at Homestead probably date from the 1870's and are excellent examples of fine woodwork of that decade.

Dr. H.H. Warburton built this home at 714–715 Main Street in 1886, using the lower floor for office and pharmacy. As Santa Clara's first physician, he began practicing in 1848.

Another home-office combination was owned by Dr. Paul at 1116 Washington.

The handsome Menzel home at 1191 Benton is representative of the Queen Anne style variations from the 1890's that abound in Santa Clara.

A beautifully maintained block of 1890's houses on Harrison, between Washington and Main, are typical of the late 19th century.

Ornate and dramatic, the Charles Morse home at the corner of Fremont and Washington, was the home of the founder of a seed company that became Ferry-Morse in the 1930's. Across the street at 1179 Washington is the 1905 Franck house, typical of the era.

The area between Santa Clara and San Jose known as *College Park* encompassed residential subdivisions from the 1870's; and the area known as University Grounds, established in 1866, developed around the University of Pacific, established here in 1870. Now Bellarmine College Preparatory, the original structures from U.O.P. days are the 1909 Helen Guth Hall, 1915 Seaton Hall, and 1910 gymnasium, all located off **Elm Street, corner of Emory**. Nearby on **University at Myrtle** is a fine Italianate-style home from the 1880's.

Where **Chapman and Morse Streets meet at Idaho and Newhall**, there are charming late-century structures from the Chapman-Davis subdivision known as Poplar City.

North of Santa Clara on **Montague Road**, Agnew State Hospital was established by the California Legislature in 1885 as a neuro-psychiatric institution for care and treatment of the mentally ill. The buildings were completed in 1888, but during the 1906 earthquake the wards collapsed, killing 112 patients. Reopened in 1911, it has been expanded and divided into two facilities.

The German Elim Church, standing at Monroe and Homestead, *originally housed the Advent-Christian congregation and was built in 1904 by Joseph Neal of Oakland.*

At 1041 Morse Street, the oldest Quaker Meeting House in California, built in 1885, is still being used by the Society of Friends. It was moved to this location from the path of the adjacent freeway in 1958.

"Let me purchase a few acres overlooking the valley, and with a distant gleam of the bay. Let me build a cottage embowered in accacia and eucalyptus."

Bayard Taylor 1859

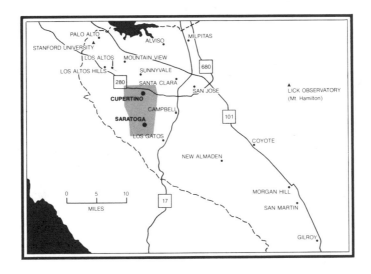

Saratoga ❧ Cupertino

In September of 1855 the *Alta California* noted that "a town McCartysville has sprung into existence, 12 miles west of San Jose at the base of the Santa Cruz Mountains."

The little village was devised by Martin McCarty, a former U. S. Army wagonmaster who had made $20,000 in the California gold fields in 1849. Figuring that a town was likely to evolve at the mouth of the canyon below William Campbell's flourishing sawmill, in 1850 McCarty took up 320 acres there of what he *supposed* was government land. Along Saratoga Creek, then called both Campbell's Creek and Arroyo Quito, he built a road to the mill, put up a toll gate and laid out his town, which was thereafter variously known as Toll Gate, McCartysville, and Bank Mills.

A settler's war nearly erupted in 1865, when the district court approved long disputed boundaries which included McCartysville and much of the surrounding land as part of nearby

Rancho Quito. The property owners either had to vacate or repurchase their land from the Arguello family, successors to the original grantees. The McCarty family obviously had too much to lose, so they purchased 128 acres from the Arguellos.

The grant was originally known as Rancho Tito for the neophyte Indian who had been in charge of Mission Santa Clara's dairy ranch located in this area in the 1830's. However, when in 1841 former mission teacher Jose Zenon Fernandez and his son-in-law Jose Noriega received the grant it was referred to as "Quito," as was the creek which runs diagonally through the center of the 13,000-acre rancho.

McCartysville was destined soon to change from a lumber town to a famous resort center. A mineral spring lying near the creek a mile above town was discovered to have chemical properties

Saratoga's Lumber Street (Big Basin Way) in 1894 looking west.

nearly identical to New York's popular Saratoga Springs. In 1864 a group of San Francisco business men purchased 720 acres surrounding the springs, built a 14-room hotel and guest cottages. Patterned after a New York spa, Pacific Congress Springs opened on June 16, 1866 amid much fanfare and a grand ball. The townspeople, realizing where their future lay, had officially adopted the fashionable name Saratoga a year earlier.

For almost 40 years until it burned to the ground in 1903 Congress Springs attracted people to Saratoga. Fortunately the town retained its peaceful charm, since it was off the railroad route and was reached only by stage from Santa Clara and Los Gatos. During these years the Saratoga Village Improvement Association purchased 500 acres of property for development,

planted orchards, and planned 10-acre subdivisions which were purchased for summer estates by the artistic set in San Francisco. The wine industry found a small niche in Saratoga's pastoral setting, and in the 1880's a former flour mill became the headquarters of the Saratoga Wine Company, a cooperative association of local vine growers that existed until the turn of the century.

In 1904 the Interurban Railway's Blossom Line connecting San Jose, Campbell, Los Gatos, and Saratoga, came at last to threaten Saratoga's somnolence. But the beautiful spot remained for another 50 years nearly as it was described in a 1911 brochure, "a charming little village in the western foothills at the entrance to the famous Congress Springs Canyon. Its freedom from saloons and their attendant evils, its good schools and superior class of people have made it attractive to people of refinement and taste."

Hannah McCarthy's summer house on Lomita Avenue at the end of Aloha Street.

Hannah McCarthy's Summer House

20600 Lomita Avenue, Saratoga

There are no McCartys left in McCartysville, as Saratoga was called in its early years. However, hidden upon a hill above town there is a house that belonged to the widow of the town's founder. It is an authentic country cottage set amid an old-fashioned flower garden.

Pretty, dark-haired Hannah Barry had come from Ireland to San Jose when she was just 17. Within 10 months she met and married Martin McCarty. They moved into a little frame house (no longer standing) on today's Big Basin Way, near the toll gate her husband had erected on the road to Campbell's mill. Enmeshed in litigation over his holdings, in May of 1853 McCarty signed over all his property to his wife, including all interest in the toll gate, and established her as a "sole trader" in a "boarding and eating house" situated at "McCarty's Stand." (Hannah later changed her name to "McCarthy.") Hannah declared she intended to engage in the purchasing and selling of livestock, real and personal property, and general trading. She then named Martin her "lawful attorney."

In 1869 it was Hannah who finally settled their land dispute with the Arguellos for $3,000. Martin McCarty, only 39, had died in 1864 leaving his young wife with three children and enough money to carry on a successful stock farm and orchard business. She also acquired several real estate holdings outside of Saratoga.

Hannah Barry was only 17 when she came from Ireland to the Santa Clara Valley and married Martin McCarty. Later when a widow, she changed the spelling to McCarthy.

One of the parcels Hannah bought was in Hollister. In the mid-1870's she took her family to live there temporarily. Her eldest son William, and daughter Margaret, married into Hollister families. After a few years Hannah decided to return to Saratoga; Margaret and her husband took over the Hollister property. In 1877 Hannah brought her younger son Daniel back to Saratoga and built the Lomita Avenue cottage.

By 1877 Saratoga was booming. It boasted a paper mill, a pasteboard mill, several saloons, and one of the most popular resorts in the West, Pacific Congress Springs. McCarty's former toll road—rechristened the Saratoga and Pescadero Turnpike—had been improved and extended past the resort and over the summit to Santa Cruz County. A popular stage line traversed its length and offered "unequaled scenery and the most breathtaking view in the state" to its passengers.

Mrs. McCarthy still owned a hundred acres in Saratoga when she built the cottage in the midst of her large vineyard in 1877. Eight squared pillars front the house which is a mixture of styles popular in the 1870's. The gabled roof lacks the jigsaw trim of the earlier Gothic style; the off-center entrance suggests a picturesque villa.

According to Hannah's granddaughter, Fannie Wilson, who lived with her off and on for several years, the busy widow McCarthy used it mainly as a summer house, while the original McCarty house six blocks away on Lumber Street (now Big Basin Way) was her "town house" where she ran the family business affairs. Margaret Wilson and her family often stayed in the house when they visited from Hollister. In fact, the youngest child Robert was born there in 1882.

Five years later Hannah McCarthy retired and sold most of her property to the Saratoga and Los Gatos Real Estate Associates (known to townsfolk as "The Syndicate"). Her younger son Dan married Lizzie Marsh, a Saratoga girl, the following year, and moved to Hollister where Dan, in partnership with his mother, became the proprietor of the Hollister Transfer Company. In Saratoga, Hannah and Dan were also partners in a commercial enterprise just down the street from the town house where Hannah spent her last years. When Hannah died in 1893, leaving a sizeable estate, William had returned to Saratoga to live with his wife Mary, son Ed, and daughters Mary and Grace. (Like his father, William died young, just four years after Hannah). Dan was divorced with no children; he and his sister Margaret and her family remained in Hollister. In the 1950's Martin McCarty's original house was torn down. All that remains of Saratoga's founding family are two commercial buildings on Big Basin Way and Hannah McCarthy's old summer house.

E. T. King House (Oriental Hotel) and Pettis Livery Stable

14605 Big Basin Way, Saratoga

There are a half dozen fascinating tales connected with this jewel of a house, and, even though many of them can't be proved, the house's character and charm alone would qualify it for anyone's list of outstanding historical houses. Most of the credit must go to decorator Barbara Caldwell, who bought the house in 1958 when it was the neighborhood wreck. A look at "before" pictures strikes one with disbelief that this once ugly duckling is the stylish house of today.

Mrs. Caldwell recognized the basically good lines of the old two-story redwood frame house. She removed the dilapidated front porch, replaced the turn-of-the-century windows with the original six-pane ones (which had been stored in the livery stable at the rear of the house), gave the place a coat of fresh paint and ended up with a fine modified Georgian farmhouse. In fact, as Mrs. Caldwell has pointed out, it is related in general form to the earlier Wythe house in Williamsburg, Virginia.

The age of the house has long been the subject of conjecture. A former owner claimed to have seen the original deed "on goatskin" dated in the 1850's. The foundation timbers, reportedly of handhewn redwood, and the compact, low-ceilinged floor plan with one large central fireplace suggests an extremely early date. However, reliable residents of Saratoga in years past recalled its construction around 1876. The earliest occupant has been mentioned as either wagonmaker-blacksmith John Chisholm, or Saratoga's most successful industrialist, Erwin T. King.

King was a New Yorker who had made a fortune in mining in the Nevada territory in the early 1860's and was proprietor of the Miners Foundry in San Francisco when he moved to Saratoga to open the Saratoga Paper Mills in 1868. He purchased 10 acres of land along Lumber Street (Big Basin Way) and invested $50,000 in the paper mill. At first he lived in Senator Charles Maclay's house at Bank Mills, half a mile west of Saratoga. When in 1874 King's company merged with Lick Mills near Agnew he moved his family there, while his brother William managed the Saratoga mill. Deeds to the property indicate King never actually owned the parcel of land where Mrs. Caldwell's house now stands. The paper mill was across Big Basin Way and around the rise that is still known as Paper Mill Hill. He may have rented the house from John Chisholm, who owned this lot and another adjoining it, from 1877 to 1889. Chisholm had purchased the land from a fellow smithy, D. C. Abbott. If the house predates 1876 a clue to its origin may lie in a quitclaim deed granted to Abbott in 1873 from Levi Millard, McCartysville's first postmaster and 1871 proprietor of the first Saratoga stage line which ran out Big Basin Way and over the summit to Santa Cruz. Millard had purchased several McCartysville lots, including this one, in 1869.

Perhaps Millard built the house as a stage stop hotel along the scenic but dangerous Big Trees Route on Big Basin Way (then called the Saratoga-Pescadero Turnpike). When Mrs. Caldwell purchased the house it was still divided into ten small hotel-like chambers, gaslights lit the unheated rooms, and the plumbing facilities were all outdoors. The well worn, steep wooden stairway to the second floor suggests heavy use over many years' service as a hotel (and, according to local gossip, a short period as a bawdy house—but we're ahead of our story).

The Saratoga Paper Mill continued to be the town's major industry throughout the 1870's and the King brothers two of its most substantial citizens. By 1880 Erwin King and his family had returned to Saratoga and were apparently living in the house in question. Production at the mill had begun to slow down and there were many complaints about the responsibility for the mill's pollution of Saratoga Creek.

Then one quiet Sunday evening in mid-April 1883, the paper mill suddenly caught fire. Within two hours the entire plant was totally destroyed—its 300-ton stacks of straw a pile of ashes. Newspapers reported the fire was "believed to have been the work of an incendiary," but no charges were brought. The Kings were understandably distraught; 15 years of work developing the mill were completely wiped out by the fire, and the Kings' hopes and fortunes as well. E. T. King's health began to fail. He took a room at the Commercial Hotel in San Francisco and one afternoon drove out to Harbor View on the Bay apparently to take a thera-

Decorator Barbara Caldwell has restored the E. T. King house at 14605 Big Basin Way.

peutic saltwater bath. Twenty feet off shore he fell forward in the sea, the victim of a heart attack. Pulled out almost immediately, he died within minutes. Back in Saratoga, people thought he died of a broken heart.

Erwin King's family moved from Saratoga shortly thereafter but his brother William, stunned with grief, remained, a sympathetic figure going daily to an improvised office—with no business to transact.

John Chisholm took over the E. T. King house again, and added a saloon to his enterprises. It was apparently during this period that the house became a boarding house of questionable reputation. Along with other rakish ac-

tivities, a lottery was run by "Pegleg" Anderson, the barkeep who worked for Chisholm. The place appears to have returned to respectability as the Oriental House, a stage stop hotel from 1893 to 1903. M. E. Pettis was the proprietor, while W. W. Pettis ran the Santa Clara Stage Line, using the handsome old barn in the rear for maintaining his stage stock.

A spotty career as a boarding house, summer home, and residence followed, while the structure fell into disrepair, until it was restored by Mrs. Caldwell in 1958.

Paul Masson's Mountain Winery*

Reached by private road off Pierce Road, Saratoga

Every summer, hundreds of music lovers gather for the Music in the Vineyards Concerts held at Paul Masson's stone winery high in the hills above Saratoga. It was here in 1896 that the Champagne King of California began his own wine operation some years after the death of his father-in-law, pioneer California vintner Charles LeFranc.

Researching Masson's career reads like a press agent's dream, and the ebullient Frenchman was his own best press agent. Everything was done with Gallic style—wine, women, and song with press releases to prove it. It is not clear who had "1852" carved in wood over the medieval arch that serves as the entranceway to the sandstone winery, but Paul Masson undoubtedly would have approved adopting what is actually the date of the establishment of Charles LeFranc's Almaden Vineyard several miles away in west San Jose.

After a short lived partnership with his brother-in-law, Henry LeFranc, Paul Masson bought out Henry's share in the Almaden Vineyard. It was there in 1892 that his first champagne was introduced. But after 1896 it was here in Saratoga at "La Cresta," as he called the spot, that Masson centered his champagne production; other wines were developed at the Almaden operation.

Here at La Cresta on a knoll above the winery he built his party house, dubbed The Chateau. This is where Paul Masson's reputation as an unrivaled host was earned. His wife, Louise was a prohibitionist and obviously wouldn't have attended the lavish dinner parties held at The Chateau. Here also is where actress Anna Held is reported to have taken her notorious and much publicized champagne bath. It is still used as a party house by the present corporation owners.

The sandstone winery was rebuilt after the 1906 earthquake, making use of sandstone blocks from the Saratoga Wine Company's building on Big Basin Way, also wrecked in the quake. At the same time the ancient entrance portal, reported to be medieval and originally imported from Spain for use in St. Patrick's Church in San Jose, was added to the structure. The winery today is seldom used for grape crushing, although the old press is there. The handsome building serves for the most part as an aging cellar for small casks of dessert wine.

---

* State Registered Landmark #733

Paul Masson's mountain winery, La Cresta, in the hills above Saratoga.

One of Senator Phelan's huge parties breaks up and the crowd fans out across the lawn at Villa Montalvo.

At Villa Montalvo—The hills go down to the east and the hills go up to the west, and here between bay and ocean is a place where man can rest. George Sterling

Villa Montalvo

End of Montalvo Road, Saratoga

One of the last of the great estates that once dotted the Santa Clara countryside, Villa Montalvo, a magnificent Mediterranean mansion with surrounding estate, stands as an appropriate memorial to James Duval Phelan, for many years considered "the foremost citizen of California."

Son of an ambitious Irish immigrant who came to San Francisco during the gold rush and made a fortune as a trader, merchant, and banker, Phelan was the epitome of a somewhat unusual American phenomenon, the California Irish gentry. Young James, born to the privileged world of great wealth, was to become mayor of San Francisco and a United States Senator. A "man of taste and learning" who would have preferred to be a poet, Phelan deferred to the wishes of his father and gave up his literary aspirations to become a partner in the family real estate and banking business, in time more than doubling its assests.

Cora (Mrs. Fremont) Older, wife of the crusading San Francisco newpaper editor and herself a noted writer, remembered James Phelan as San Francisco's greatest host after the death of banker William Ralston. According to her, Phelan was "the city's most eligible bachelor," who financed talented California playwrights, artists, and sculptors, filling Montalvo with their creations. "There never was anyone like him," she claimed.

During his three terms as mayor of San Francisco, Phelan created a new city charter, instituted public ownership of utilities and many other farsighted reforms. He has been pictured as a Renaissance prince of the Victorian age who used his fortune to lead California to greatness. But two years of labor troubles plagued Mayor Phelan's third term and he did not run again.

The Olders and Phelan decided to buy some property in the sun-splashed Santa Clara Valley. Their plans were for something rustic—much like the ranch Cora and Fremont Older were to build a few miles from Montalvo. Phelan at first envisioned "a little box in the country," which would eventually prove to be majestic Villa Montalvo, named for the sixteenth century Spanish writer who first coined the name "California."

In 1911, having abandoned plans to join forces with the Olders, James Phelan purchased 160 acres in the Saratoga foothills and embarked upon his Villa Montalvo project, which was remarkbly elaborate even for those pretentious times. Like other wealthy Californians he was probably looking forward to entertaining European guests during the upcoming Panama-Pacific International Exposition of 1915.

Construction was begun on the 19-room mansion in 1912. As supervising architect, Phelan had chosen William Curlett a designer of one early version of San Francisco's pre-quake City Hall as well as, appropriately the Phelan Building in that city. Upon Curlett's death in January 1914 his son Alex Curlett and their partner Charles E. Gottschalk took over the completion of the sandstone Villa Montalvo. John McLaren, Golden Gate Park's great landscape designer, laid out the grounds replete with hidden nooks and wisteria-covered pergolas.

Phelan was off in Europe promoting international participation in the 1915 Fair and selecting from Europe's finest art treasures for his mansion and gardens. In Granada he purchased the splendid antique carved wooden doors that stand at the entry. He even arranged for a fine Italian craftsman to come to Montalvo to carve a variety of honey-toned woods—Georgian eucalyptus in the lofty arched hallway, Circassian walnut for the adjoining library walls. Here paintings by California's most noted artists were to be hung along with those of Peel and Domergue.

Late in 1914 the doors to Villa Montalvo opened to the first of many celebrated guests. That same year James Duval Phelan became the first United States Senator from California to be elected by popular vote. He took office in March of 1915 and served with apparent distinction in Washington, D. C., until 1921 when he, a Democrat, was defeated amid the Republican landslide that put Warren Harding in office.

After nearly two years traveling around the world Senator Phelan returned to Montalvo where he indulged

In March 1915 Vice President Thomas W. Marshall (in the wicker chair) was entertained at Villa Montalvo by Senator James D. Phelan (to Marshall's right). The party, which included Secretary of the Navy Franklin D. Roosevelt (front row, 6th from right), were at Montalvo during a weekend break from the Exposition in San Francisco.

his party-loving penchant to the fullest. He seemed to crave the company of the artistically accomplished, especially those who had brought fame to his native state, much as in his earlier San Francisco years he had enjoyed the stylish Telegraph Hill salons frequented by the city's bohemians.

Novelist Gertrude Atherton, Phelan's constant companion of later years, had her own room in the Villa at the top of the stairs. For 15 years she was the honored guest at many of Phelan's lavish house parties. In his last years James Phelan's favorite guest was the beautiful young tennis star Helen Wills, according to Mrs. Atherton; she said he showered attention on the statuesque six-time Wimbledon champion who had brought worldwide notice to California. Still, Gertrude Atherton maintained she was sure that Phelan loved California more than any human being.

Phelan's death at Villa Montalvo on August 7, 1930 was followed by the "largest and most imposing funeral ever seen in San Francisco," according to newspaper accounts. His multimillion dollar estate was generously apportioned among all those he loved. The two largest bequests were a million dollars to establish the James D. Phelan Foundation, the income to be expended solely for charitable purposes to the poor. The other was the gift of Villa Montalvo to the San Francisco Art Association along with $250,000, the income of which was to be used to maintain the property as a public park. The buildings and grounds were to be used as far as possible for the development of art, literature, music, and architecture by promising students.

After standing dark for many years after Phelan's death, Villa Montalvo at last does serve as a center for the arts under the sponsorship of the Montalvo Association. Today, resident artists live and work on the magnificent estate as envisioned years ago by the imaginative, generous James Duval Phelan.

One of Willis Polk's most outstanding structures, the Blaney villa on Rancho Bella Vista.

Rancho Bella Vista—The Blaney Villa

On a Private Road, Saratoga

Seldom does a house, or a mansion, live up to one's expectations, but the Mediterranean villa the versatile Willis Polk created for the Charles Blaneys certainly does. One easily agrees with the critic who in *The Architectural Record* (February 1918) exclaimed, "It strikes me as the most enchanting structure I've ever seen, and therefore may not be there when I go back."

By 1917 when the house was built, the architect, Willis Polk, was at the height of his career. He had developed a successful formula for creating suitable residences for the rich, usually by interpreting a period style—in this case late Renaissance and 16th century villa architecture—in a free and highly personal way. The buff pink tone of the exterior and the muted grey roof tiles are extremely effective in conveying timelessness to the villa.

Unlike many of their neighbors whose country estates were merely weekend showplaces, the Blaneys lived full time in their home, which helps explain one of the more remarkable things about the interior of the house—its human proportions. It is eminently livable in spite of its size of nearly 20 rooms and a floor plan that is rambling and complicated. The Blaney's personal room requirements were constantly considered as well as the natural features of the site—the view of the surrounding countryside, the slope of the land, the old trees, an old well from the days when a frame ranch house belonging to Mrs. Blaney's pioneer relatives had occupied the site.

Her cousins, the John Farwell family, who had originally called the place "Rancho Bella Vista" came to Saratoga in 1856 and located on 160 acres of government land. After John Farwell died

Rancho Bella Vista's original house shown here in the 1870's, belonged to the John Farwell family, relatives of the Charles Blaneys.

Cupertino

If vineyards gave but a small boost to sleepy Saratoga's existence, they were the life blood of Cupertino. Captain Elisha Stevens, leader of the 1844 Stevens-Murphy-Townsend Party across the Sierra was the area's earliest viniculturist; in 1848 he settled on Cupertino Creek, later renamed for him. After leaving his imprint on the creek and a major roadway, the captain left his Blackberry Farm around 1860, when the valley reportedly had become too crowded for his taciturn taste. In the 1870's his farm was developed as a resort and enjoyed great popularity for many years.

Dozens of viniculturists, many of them retired sea captains, followed the trail along Stevens Creek Road and in 1882 the Cupertino post office was established on McClelland Road at John T. Doyle's Las Palmas Winery. The post office took its name from the original Spanish designation for the creek, Arroyo de San José Cupertino.

In the late 1890's, deadly grape parasites attacked the once prosperous vineyards, destroying most of the vines. A decade later Cupertino became a center for horse breeding as well as an orchard-surrounded stop on the old Blossom Line streetcar route, which was discontinued in 1932. Along with most of the Santa Clara Valley the "West Side," as it was once known, remained unchanged until the suburban population explosion of the 1960's.

in 1866 his son Franklin and daughter Jennie, ran the ranch until 1905 when Blaney purchased it.

When Governor Hiram Johnson was elected, he appointed Charles Blaney, a personal friend, to the first State Highway Commission in 1911. Blaney and the other two commissioners conducted a 6,000-mile tour of the state and were largely responsible for establishing California's road system. Mr. Blaney retired because of ill health the same year the villa was completed. Later residents included his nephew Robert Kirkwood, prominent civic official and California State Controller at the time of his death in 1964.

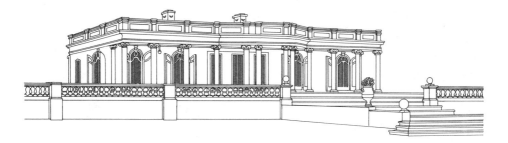

Willis Polk designed Beaulieu for Charles Baldwin and his wife, Virginia, to stand at the top of the stairway and garden pool where Flint Center Theatre is now.

Miraflores—Beaulieu (The "Petit Trianon")

At De Anza College, Cupertino

Until the restoration of this once beautiful house is completed (a 1976 Bicentennial project of the City of Cupertino and the Trianon Foundation) it is better to read of it as it was in 1902 when featured in *House and Garden*:

> Nestled close to the entrance of a great canon [sic], in the uplands of the Santa Clara Valley, is a vineyard of some seventy acres. From the vineyard proper, in all directions for miles, blooms one vast orchard. The central gem in this unique natural setting is Beaulieu, the home of Mr. C. A. Baldwin. It is essentially a vineyard. A drive of palms leads to the grounds, which are laid out after eighteenth century models. On ascending two flights of steps from the drive, one is not surprised to find a pavilion after the style which the French borrowed from the Italian. The pure whiteness of the Ionic order contrasts with the dark green of the foliage and the unfailing blue of the sky . . . .

The pavilion the writer spoke of is the "Petit Trianon," an incorrect name of unknown origin. The owners, Charles and Ella Baldwin, called the estate Beaulieu. Baldwin bottled his wine under that label. And their residence, designed by San Francisco architect Willis Polk, resembled in a vaguely modern way the columned one-story Grand Trianon at Versailles (in miniature) rather than the two-storied Petit Trianon. It looks, indeed, like something appropriate to contemporary Beverly Hills rather than 1900 Cupertino. Baldwin originally called the place (which he purchased in 1887) Miraflores, before his marriage in 1896 to the beautiful and rich Ella Hobart, daughter of a Comstock silver tycoon. There is no evidence that they ever referred to their home as Le Petit Trianon.

"About 1900" appears to be the most likely date of construction of the house, although it may be as early as 1896, according to an architect researching the work of Willis Polk. In the early

1890's, Polk, the "*enfant terrible* of western architecture" led the return to Period design that swept California. Willis Polk, as a good Period architect, occasionally used variants of classicizing Baroque. Beaulieu is a valid example of that style. It also captured the European spirit simulated in other centers of California viniculture.

The folks around West Side (Cupertino) called Charles Baldwin, who was their first millionaire, "Admiral" as a title of respect. An elegant, "stiff backed" polo player, he was actually the son of Rear-Admiral Charles H. Baldwin, who had once captained Commodore Vanderbilt's yacht. The English-educated younger Charles had never served in the Navy, had never, apparently, done any work until at the age of 26 he purchased the 70 acres in Cupertino and turned it into a productive vineyard. He installed a massive stone winery and underground cellars (still on the college grounds) and set out vines from the Bordeaux and Graves regions of France. His Beaulieu wines were sold in New York, London, and Central America.

The Baldwins were leaders of San Francisco's "Fast Set" according to chronicles of the city's society in the 1890's. In addition to their estate at Cupertino where they gave extravagant parties, they had a country home near her family's place in Burlingame.

Shortly after the turn of the century Mrs. Baldwin became a victim of tuberculosis and spent several years in a wheelchair. Because of her health, the Baldwin's purchased property in Colorado Springs and commissioned the eminent New York architect, Stanford White, to design a larger country villa they called Claremont, patterned once again after Louis XIV's Grand Trianon. In 1908 they moved to Colorado (where Mrs. Baldwin did totally recover), taking their exquisite antique French furnishings and sixteenth century art collection with them. The following year they sold Beaulieu to their friend, Francis J. Carolan, another San Francisco millionaire socialite. The Carolans lived here off and on for several years while, in 1915, building a fabulous 92-room French chateau in Burlingame. It may have been Mrs. Carolan, an ardent Francophile, who dubbed Beaulieu "Le Petit Trianon," perhaps referring to its size as "petit" rather than its architectural origin.

Since 1965 the Baldwin's former estate has become the site of De Anza Community College. Remnants of the gardens remain; the winery is there, as are the guest cottages. The lovely house has twice been jacked up and moved, first to make way for the Flint Center (theatre) and next yielding to that ever-constant threat to historical buildings, the parking lot. The classical columns have tumbled, the walls have cracked, it appears to the uninitiated to be almost beyond repair—but the Trianon Foundation is determined that it be restored to serve as a museum and collection center for California memorabilia.

Mrs. Baldwin, the beautiful silver heiress Virginia Hobart, in a 1910 painting by Louis Mark.

This redwood and bamboo Moon-Gate marks the entrance to "Hakone" Japanese gardens, now a city park at 21000 Big Basin Way. The gate and tea house were brought from the 1915 Exposition in San Francisco. Isabel Stine developed this property in 1918, hiring Japanese artisans to build the main house and guest cottages in traditional style.

The two-story Classical-Federal home at 20375 Saratoga-Los Gatos Road that was built in 1911 for the C.A. Wood family was known as "Woodleigh" and is now an antique shop.

Supplement

Saratoga ■ Cupertino

Saratoga

Saratoga maintains a village atmosphere by encouraging re-use of older downtown structures. A few have had to be relocated as with the McWilliams cottage, moved to a new site on the **Saratoga-Los Gatos Road** behind the village library. Both the cottage and the false-front store relocated adjacent to it will eventually be restored and used together as a museum.

The general store and butcher shop buildings that still stand on either side of **Third Street alley**, west side of Big Basin, were built in the 1880's and have 10-inch thick walls of stone. The old store-post office-bakery at **14471 Big Basin**, now the Clef House, is an excellent prospect for restoration. Old photos prove that it was one of Saratoga's handsomest buildings when built by Hannah McCarthy and son Dan circa 1890. Another McCarthy-built structure at **14519 Big Basin Way** is now called the Kocher Building.

The home of the west valley's first orchardist, J. P. Springer, stands on a knoll above Fourth Street's **Wildwood Park**. The frame structure is said to have been built of pre-cut lumber, shipped from New England. Springer arrived in 1841 with the Bidwell & Bartleson party, first American immigrants to journey overland to Alta California.

The 1895 Methodist-Episcopal Church at **20490 Saratoga-Los Gatos Road**, after undergoing several exterior changes and uses, is now an antique shop. Several offices and shops along **Big Basin Way** were old homes. At the corner of **Sixth Street** stands the 1869 Henry house and at **14503** is Sam Cloud's home from the 1880's.

Three 1870's redwood frame houses are easily seen. Two are on **Saratoga Avenue**: the Dresser home, at **14300**, and the Mason home at **14005**. The house of Saratoga Paper Mill's co-founder, W. T. King, at **14672 Oak Street** has been nicely maintained though remodeled from its original form.

Several houses from the 1880's are the Fabretti cottage at **14669 Big Basin Way**, the Congregational Church parsonage at **14660 Oak Street**, and the Crowell home at **19855 Douglass Lane**. The residence that J. B. Ellis built in 1880 at **14711 Fruitvale**, called "Old Orchard," was heavily remodeled in 1938 but still retains its New England farmhouse charm.

Garrod's Ranch on **Mt. Eden Road** was established as an orchard in the 1890's but is now a popular center for local horsemen. Another early ranch that continues to maintain a producing orchard is at the corner of **Saratoga Avenue and Fruitvale**. Initially owned by T. Reynolds, it has remained in the same family for a hundred years.

The Mission-Revival era is locally represented by the 1912 I.O.O.F. home for the aged on **Fruitvale Avenue**.

One of Saratoga's most craftsmanlike, pre-1920 homes is the redwood, two-story house built by lumberman Neil Carmichael in 1914 on the west side of **Saratoga-Sunnyvale Road at 14051**. It sits among redwood trees across from the high school. Together with his brother Dan and Thomas Hubbard, Carmichael ran a lumber mill above Saratoga from 1889 to 1911.

On the old brick portion of the Saratoga-Los Gatos Road, now called **Austin Way**, stands the 1912 Austin School, the last vestige of a once busy settlement. The nearby Nippon Mura Inn (now La Hacienda Inn) and the Los Gatos Saratoga Wine & Fruit Company Winery, located at the **Quito Road end** from 1885 to 1919, comprised the center of this settlement.

Designed by Julia Morgan, the Saratoga Foothill Clubhouse was built in 1916 on Park Place *where it still serves as a local cultural center.*

Saratoga's only cannery is now the Campbell Cage Co. at 12760 Saratoga Avenue. Built as part of the Farrington Ranch, it was later owned by "Borax" Smith and operated as the Sorosis Fruit Packing Company. It became a social center in the late 19th century.

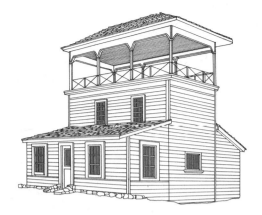

All that remains of a fine estate built by Nathan Hall in the 1880's is this tank house on Stevens Creek Boulevard near Phar Lap Road, *named for a later owner's famous race horse.*

Between Saratoga and Cupertino on Prospect Road above Stelling, *are two estates of the early 20th century. Visible from the Stelling corner is the "Painless" Parker ranch house (1916), a vacant ruin that nestles on the ridge above a palm-lined entrance road. The estate of this once-famous dentist may become future parklands. At the* top of Prospect *is the 160-acre ranch of Fremont and Cora Older, both well-known writers, who built their home called "Woodhills" in 1913. This property too is in ruins, only the writers' studio (see photo) beside the old pool is still occupied. It was built with blocks moved from an 1847 San Jose adobe that was dismantled in 1923. Fremont Older was a dynamic editor who championed social causes from 1897 to his death in 1935. He served as editor of various Hearst newspapers from 1918 on. Older commuted daily to San Francisco from his own stop, called Fremont Station, beside Stelling Road at Prospect.*

One of three remaining schools built before 1900, the old Collins School (1894) is now the Cupertino de Oro Club, on Homestead at Saratoga-Sunnyvale Road. *Two tiny one-room school houses remain. The 1867 San Antonio School, between the creek and the railroad tracks, off* North Foothill Boulevard near Maryknoll entrance road, *has been converted to a residence with additions, but it still remains at the original site. The Montebello School, high up* Montebello Road, *has been used constantly since 1892 when it was built by the Picchetti family for the children of Montebello Ridge. It will be moved to a new location to make room for a new school on this site.*

The Picchetti home and winery on Montebello Road remains as evidence of a thriving viticulture industry in early Cupertino. The Picchettis developed their acreage in the 1880's and built this charming stone winery in 1896. No longer commercial vintners, the family boards horses and slowly sells off the acreage they once tilled. Dr. Osea Perrone of San Francisco developed a vineyard which once spread over 180 acres at the top of Montebello Ridge. A pre-1890 stone cellar, covered with a wood summer house, still remains at the top of a steep eight-mile grade behind private gates and alongside a fortress-like structure (built by the doctor's nephew in the 1920's) which is visible from Montebello Road. Other pre-1920 industries include the 1914 Monta Vista Canning Company (now Woelffel Cannery) whose neat white frame structures stand on Imperial Avenue; and the Mariani Fruit Packing Company, founded in 1913. A white frame bungalow, dating from 1919, is used for an office. It is located beside the complex of buildings on Saratoga-Sunnyvale Road, between Junipero Serra Freeway and Homestead Road.

The 1890 Enoch Parrish house, on Stevens Creek Boulevard at Mary Avenue, stands boarded and waiting for restoration despite a recent fire. The tank house was built after Parrish bought the property in 1883; and the barn was built in 1906, using redwood milled in 1873 that had been part of McCauley's Blackberry Farm resort hotel until the 1906 earthquake destroyed it. Another old barn (ca. 1890's) stands on the McClellan Ranch property (located at McClellan Road beside the creek) which is now part of a recreation park. Charley Baer's 1903 family home and a replica of his father's blacksmith shop are located on Stevens Creek at Saratoga-Sunnyvale Road. The horse barn, built circa 1915 by Joseph De Laveaga, will soon be enclosed by further development of this creekside land. It stands on Stevens Creek Canyon Road across from San Juan Road.

Forbes Mill, Los Gatos

*"The climate is delightful and a slight elevation enabling
one to overlook the magnificant valley supplies a scene of which
the eye should never tire."*

The Pacific Tourist *1884*

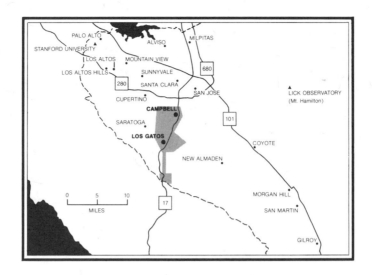

Los Gatos ❧ Campbell

Los Gatos owes its existence to James Alexander Forbes, one of the most interesting men in early California history. Forbes was an educated and intelligent Scotsman who landed in California off the whaler *Fanny* in 1831 and became the British vice-consul while California was still under Mexican rule. He was involved in a large amount of Santa Clara Valley real estate, from Palo Alto to Milpitas, from Mission Santa Clara to the Santa Cruz Range, in addition to a complicated involvement in the New Almaden Mine.

In 1850, after selling his Potrero Rancho near Santa Clara, he began construction of a stone flour mill* he called the "Santa Rosa," on Los Gatos Creek not far from the old Franciscan Mission Trail between Santa Clara and Santa Cruz. The creek and rancho on which it stood took the name Los Gatos from the wildcats in the area. It is said that Jose Hernandez, one of the grantees of this Rancho Rinconada de los Gatos, first coined the name in 1839, but when the notorious renegade Indian Yoscolo used the canyon as a hideout in the early 1830's, reports indicated that the Indians had known of La Cuesta de los Gatos from ancient times. Hernandez and his brother-in-law Sebastian Peralta had been granted the 6,631-acre rancho on May 21, 1840. After the U. S. Land Commission confirmed the rancho to them in 1854, Forbes officially recorded his purchase of 2,000 acres from Jose Hernandez. But James Alexander Forbes was unable to overcome the competition from Campbell's mill near Saratoga, and Lick and Sunol mills on the Guadalupe River, and his enterprise failed. In 1856 "Don Diego" Forbes declared bankruptcy. The lush, wooded surroundings of his mill were destined to become a town.

* State Registered Landmark #458, visible off Highway 17

When the timber stands around the mill at Lexington on the ridge above town were wooded out, many of the pioneer lumbermen came down to "Forbes Mill" and there on the banks of Los Gatos Creek established the nucleus of a town. The mill itself was successfully enlarged by William H. Rogers. By 1869 Rogers and his partners J. W. McMillan and Dr. W. S. McMurtry had formed the Los Gatos Manufacturing Company, and the town plan of Los Gatos had been filed at the County Recorder's office. The town then consisted of one long street running east and west predictably dubbed "Main Street" (as it is still known today). Highway 17 follows the original Los Gatos Creek course. Santa Cruz Avenue was then called "Lexington Road" and was the westernmost street in town. Where the town plaza is today was John Lyndon's Ten Mile House, which in 1864 housed the first post office and was the first hotel in town and later the site of the Los Gatos railroad station. In 1878 the narrow gauge South Pacific Coast Railroad was completed from Alameda (in Contra Costa County), past Milpitas and Alviso to Los Gatos (eventually extending to Santa Cruz), transforming the peaceful hamlet into a bustling village.

The Peralta-Hernandez adobe, headquarters of Rinconada de Los Gatos Rancho.

Rinconada De Los Gatos Adobe (Peralta—Hernandez)

Los Gatos

When a house is more than 130 years old and was once the headquarters of the fabled Peralta-Hernandez Rancho Rinconada de los Gatos, uncovering its history is like unraveling a detective yarn. The stories surrounding this large pink stucco and adobe house that sits on the east bank of San Tomas Aquino Creek are an interplay between myth and reality. Enclosed within the main living area is the adobe structure built by the original grantee—but was it Peralta or Hernandez?

Sebastian Peralta, a great gruff bear of a man, Indian fighter, official of Pueblo San Jose and onetime majordomo of Mission Santa Clara, was granted this rancho in 1840. As was often the case in early California where family ties were all important, his co-grantee was a relative, his brother-in-law Jose Hernandez. The two men were married to sisters of the Cibrian family of San Jose. Hernandez was also a former soldier, but not a native of California as was Sebastian. (His father Pedro Peralta had come as a boy with his parents in the Anza party.*)

Peralta and Hernandez at first both lived in this area of the rancho with their families, and very likely with their in-laws, the Leocadio Cibrians. The original rancho map shows three adobe houses in this location about 200 feet apart. There is no way of proving which family lived in the existing adobe, the largest and only one of the three still standing. But the evidence suggests it was originally Sebastian Peralta.

After the death of his wife Maria Gregoria Cibrian, Peralta married Paula Sepulveda in 1846 and they moved to the northern tip of the grant, near today's Campbell. He was living there when Fremont's battalion camped on the rancho on their way to Santa Cruz a few months before the Bear Flag Revolt in June 1846. Peralta went to Fremont's bivouac and claimed that some of the horses the party had "acquired" were actually his and asked for payment. The Americans refused. Peralta later pressed his claim with the American authorities but to no avail.

During this period, the adobe was occupied by Jose Vicente Fernandez and his wife, Sebastian's sister, Magdelena Peralta. In 1853 Fernandez paid

Jose Hernandez one of the grantees of the Rancho and one of the owners of the adobe.

---

* See Luis Peralta's Adobe, San Jose, Chapter 8.

taxes on this adobe (which was assessed at $500). The same year Peralta sold this western part of the rancho (2,500 acres along San Tomas Aquino Creek and northwest of Los Gatos Creek) to Claude Simon. Jose Hernandez' first wife Maria Gertrudis Cibrian had also died (the Cibrian sisters' deaths undoubtedly made division of the rancho necessary). In 1853 Hernandez paid taxes on the eastern side of the grant, 3,240 acres he called "Santa Rosa Rancho." It was 2,000 acres of this section that Hernandez had contracted to sell in 1852 to James Alexander Forbes, and for which Forbes paid $8,000 on May 26, 1855, after the Land Commission had confirmed Hernandez' legal title to the rancho. Here Forbes built his mill which he also called "Santa Rosa." Hernandez and his second wife moved away to Baja, California shortly after the sale.

Local history buffs have long claimed that the Quito Road adobe was Hernandez' hacienda, and had previously been The Hunting Lodge of Governor Luis Arguello. A search of the deeds to the property gives a clue to both of these mistaken, if romantic, notions.

After Claude Simon bought the property from Peralta it passed through a series of Frenchmen's hands and was subdivided. In 1876 a 276-acre parcel which had been acquired by Thomas Blake was sold to Jose Ramon Arguello, son of the former Governor Luis, and owner of Rancho Quito just across San Tomas Aquino Creek.* After Arguello's death, his widow, Isabel Alviso de Arguello, married Frank Hernandez of Santa Clara and used the adobe as a summer home for several years. Frank Hernandez may well have been related to Jose Hernandez the rancho grantee, but there is no evidence that he had any connection with the rancho before his marriage to Don Jose Ramon Arguello's widow.

Therefore it would seem that the adobe's real Arguello and Hernandez connections have been misinterpreted and romanticized, obscuring the apparent truth that it was originally Sebastian Peralta's adobe, not Jose Hernandez.

After the turn of the century a San Francisco businessman found the adobe an abandoned derelict. Enchanted by Los Gatos' pastoral charm, he bought the adobe and 100 acres surrounding it, which included a weatherbeaten frame house and pumphouse (now gone). The one-and-a-half-story adobe was in great disrepair. Recognizing its historic value and the integrity of its style, he commissioned an authentic restoration. Despite later additions which nearly tripled its size, the mood if not the actual details of traditional adobe houses has been retained.

* See Arguello House, Chapter 5, Santa Clara. Also Chapter 6, Saratoga.

James Lyndon's house survived the move from Broadway Street to Main Street only to burn down in August of 1975.

James Lyndon House

270 East Main Street, Los Gatos

What the McCartys mean to the history of Saratoga, the Lyndons mean to Los Gatos' history. Although the house of John Lyndon, the elder of the two pioneer Los Gatos brothers, is gone, James Lyndon's multi-gabled frame house managed to survive for nearly a century.

In 1972 the house which originally stood on the corner of Santa Cruz Avenue and Broadway was jacked up and moved several blocks away to its present site. There it was given a contrasting coat of pastel paint that highlights its interesting late 19th century features. Mill-cut wood simulates shingles in the gable, there are unusual, squared corner bay windows. On the third level an "eyebrow" window peeks through the roof. The whole is a somewhat "warmed-over" variant on late Victorian forms, with four-square comfort chosen over style.

122

In this handsome house James H. Lyndon and members of his family lived from 1878 until 1964. Before building the house, which stood on part of a hundred acres John Lyndon subdivided in 1877, James, his wife Anna and James Lloyd, the eldest of their six children, had lived in Ten Mile House, a wayside inn that stood on Santa Cruz Avenue. For awhile James managed the hotel in partnership with his brother John, who not only was ten years older but apparently became ten times richer than James. According to James' biography he worked for his brother off and on for many years until at last in 1883 he "set up in the lumber business for himself."

James, who appears to have been more outgoing and popular than his business-minded brother, was elected Sheriff of Santa Clara County in 1894. In addition, he served as Los Gatos' postmaster and president of the town's board of trustees.

After the last of the Lyndons died in 1964, the building stood vacant and was due to be torn down. The present owner rescued the historic old house and moved it to East Main Street.

The McCullagh Estate, La Estancia

18000 Overlook Road, Los Gatos

In July 1900 construction was begun on this rare example of the versatile Willis Polk's work in Mission Revival Architecture. It is gratifying to be able to see a Revival house in modified "Mission" by the man who was largely responsible for the Period eclecticism that swept California architecture in the late 1890's and continued into the twentieth century.

Polk was assisted in the design by architect George Washington Percy, who is best known for his work in masonry, especially the impressive Christian Brothers Winery in Napa County, designed for Polk's great patron William Bourn. The house which was supposedly inspired by Mission San Miguel Archangel southeast of Carmel —the front of the house is somewhat like that of the mission complex— was constructed in an unorthodox manner. The contractor, J.R. Tobin, cut an existing frame ranch house in half and had it pulled apart by teams of horses. The present arcaded loggia was then built to join the two halves.

The owners who requested this unusual building project were Frank and Mary Evans McCullagh who had a sentimental attachment to the original two-story building.

The McCullaghs had come to California in 1880 hoping that California's climate would benefit Frank McCullagh's failing health (which it apparently did; he lived another 57 years to the age of 84). Then for some reason in 1887 they sold their 120-acre ranch

Frank and Mary Evans McCullagh commissioned the versatile Willis Polk and George Washington Percy to create La Estancia in the Mission Revival style that swept California in the late 1890s and early 1900s.

to Saratoga and Los Gatos Real Estate and returned to Philadelphia for seven years. In 1894 they returned and repurchased six-and-a-half acres and moved back into their old ranch house. They wanted to retain their original place and yet Mary McCullagh, who was a "great student of history," was caught up in the Mission Fever of the times.

Polk and Percy's design turned out to be "one of the most sensitive interpretations of the architecture of the Franciscan Mission," according to Professor Richard Longstreth of the University of California. The rear patio, which was added after 1939 and enclosed by graceful arched walls, is exceptional. Around the back of the house are two Della Robbia niches. Many of the windows have authentic copies of mission-period shutters.

Mary McCullagh, who called the place "La Estancia," lived here following her husband's death in 1937. She died the next year and the estate was sold to Dr. and Mrs. Horace Jones who did extensive remodeling but apparently maintained the original character of the house.

The house was nearly lost in 1974 to developers who planned to tear it down for a multi-unit condominium. But the concern of Los Gatos citizens and the enlightened action of the city council has forestalled its destruction at least temporarily under the terms of an historic zoning ordinance which was inspired by the controversy over the house. It was placed on the National Register of Historic Places in October 1974.

The Hyde-Sunsweet factory when it was a bustling canning operation in the 1920s.

Campbell

Campbell is named for Benjamin Campbell, son of William Campbell who built the first saw mill in the county and who did the first official surveys of both Santa Clara and San Jose. Benjamin was only 15 when he came with his father across the plains from Missouri in 1846. After a stint in the gold mines and assisting his father in constructing Campbell's Mill (at Saratoga) he went back to Missouri to be married. Returning in 1851 with his bride Mary, he bought a squatter's right to 150 acres, and after 18 years' litigation finally received title to it from the U. S. Government.

In 1885 Ben Campbell subdivided his land, taking advantage of his location along the route of the railroad, and he became the postmaster at Campbell Station, the town's original designation.

The place was first an active grain-producing center but as the valley's orchards expanded, fruit canneries took over as the major enterprise. In the early 1900's local newspapers touted Campbell as "The Orchard City," and proudly called attention to the fact that founding father Ben Campbell had seen to it that this was a dry town—every deed carried the restriction that no liquor could be sold there.

The Great Depression of the 1930's, coupled with overproduction of the bountiful orchards, caused economic disaster for Campbell as with many of the agriculturally dependent valley towns, 90 percent of the Santa Clara Valley farms were reported mortgaged before World War II. Since the postwar land boom, Campbell's orchards and farms have virtually disappeared. But here and there amid the acres of suburban homes, one can glimpse remnants of the vast fruit ranches that once surrounded Campbell.

The Hyde–Sunsweet Factory

93 Central Avenue, Campbell

The little town that began as Campbell's Station back in 1885 has had its ups and downs through the years. Its history follows the boom-and-bust pattern of many valley towns as it changed from the center of the Santa Clara Valley's fruit industry to a little-known stop on the Southern Pacific line to Santa Cruz.

The strongest link with its heyday as a major fruit drying center is the six-acre, former Sunsweet factory sitting at the south end of Central Avenue. Recently after months of construction work the huge old brick and redwood facility has been transformed into a re-creationally oriented shopping complex, appropriately dubbed "The Factory."

In 1891 a group of Campbell orchardists established a farmers' cooperative. The following year they purchased 16 acres of land at the south end of Central Avenue and the Campbell Fruit Growers Union Drying Plant was born. The $30,000 facility had a capacity of curing 7,000 tons of fruit a year. The company stock was entirely owned by the fruit growers themselves, each share of stock entitling its owner to have an acre of fruit processed.

Then in 1909, California pioneer George E. Hyde bought the Fruit Growers Union acreage and converted the plant to a canning and dehydrating facility. Campbell had become a center of the valley's fruit industry—wide-spreading orchards, watered by a network of irrigating canals radiating from Los Gatos Creek, checkerboarded the countryside. In time, the entire Santa Clara valley became a mass of fruit orchards. Disease had destroyed the burgeoning wine industry years earlier, and one by one the vineyards converted to the heartier fruit varieties.

Eventually markets became scarce and the cannery business was threatened by overproduction as well as the Depression. The prune, however, had become one of California's most important fruits. The California Prune and Apricot Association, called "Sunsweet," purchased the Hyde facility and in 1937 established their major prune dehydrating factory there. Sunsweet used the facility until 1971.

The historic industrial plant, at one time the largest fruit drying plant in the world, once again is the hub of activity in Campbell. The original 1892 fruit warehouse has been converted into retail shops, as has one large frame building which once served as the receiving and preparing shed. (The other brick buildings and sheds date from 1910 to 1920 and were built by the Hydes as part of their Sunnyside canning operation.)

With layers of paint removed, the Hofstra Block, at the corner of Main and Santa Cruz, *looks nearly the same as it did in 1895. Nearby at the corner of* Main and Montebello *is the Rankin Building, (ca. 1902) which housed the Post Office from 1917–1948. Across the street at* 140 West Main, *Ford's Opera House, built in 1904, now houses several antique shops.*

The unusual Richardson Romanesque brick house, with rough cut stone trim, was built by Harry Perrin for his bride in 1895. At 315 University, *it is now used for offices. A simpler, related structure at the corner of* University and West Main, *the Fretwell Building was contstructed in 1906 and was used by the First National Bank from 1912 to 1918. A 1918 building used by the same bank was recently restored by Homestead Savings at* 160 West Main.

Supplement

Los Gatos ∎ Campbell

Los Gatos

Although much remodeled, the old Toll House at **142 South Santa Cruz at Wood Road** has been here since 1867 when James Kennedy operated a toll gate on the new county road that ran behind his house and across the Santa Cruz grade. Used for only ten years, it then became a boarding house and is now an antique shop.

Late 19th-century homes abound in Los Gatos. From the late 1880's into the early century, the west valley town experienced a home building boom. **Fairview Plaza**, **Glen Ridge Avenue, and Hernandez**, as well as other streets close by, contain some of Los Gatos' finest houses from this period. Historically notable is the home of George Hooke, who bought the Los Gatos Fruit Company in 1894 and sold it to Hunt Brothers in 1906. The porch which surrounds the house at **25 Glen Ridge** has been partially filled in with room expansions but is otherwise little changed from the original design believed to have been drawn by Bernard Maybeck in the late 1890's. Its neighbor from 1885 at **33 Glen Ridge** has maintained a scalloped shingle character despite additions and the modernization of windows. The carriage house at the rear is still used. The house's most famous resident was John Crummey, founder of the Food Machinery Corporation.

At **45 Broadway** is a charming restoration of an 1875 Italianate home.

There are good cottage restorations in the area of **Massol and Bachman Avenues**, evidence of a growing trend to preserve sound old structures in their excellent location in the downtown area.

The corner of **Miles and Edelan Avenue** has two beautifully preserved Queen Anne residences. The A. Skinkle, Jr., house at **129 Edelan** has a fine carriage house, and the Miles home at **130 Edelan** features a curved porch and a scallop-shingled tower.

Among several attractive homes on the east end of Main Street, going up **Loma Alta, Johnson and Alpine**, is another interesting restoration at **75 Alpine**, the 1885 Moser house. Mrs. Moser was a friend of Sarah Winchester, a frequent visitor. The carriage house adjacent has become a separate residence. Nearby at **107 Foster Road** is the Herman Sund home built by the Swedish immigrant in 1884. At **122 Los Gatos Boulevard** is a nicely restored cottage, once the summer house of Alma Spreckels of San Francisco. Not far from here at **42 Central Avenue** the well known Florentine Village has existed since 1887 as a home, winery, and more recently a restaurant.

Two 1870's "school cottages" were private homes where classes were held at **179 Loma Alta** and **269 Los Gatos Boulevard**.

The 1875 home of Peter Johnson remains at **49 Los Gatos Boulevard**. A native of Denmark, Johnson arrived in the county in 1861 and was the chairman of Los Gatos' Board of Trustees in 1892–94, when the town had only 1645 residents.

Unusual for Los Gatos is the Oriental-styled home built in 1909 at **16600 Cypress Way** by Senator Sanborn Young and his wife, author and poet, Ruth Comfort Mitchell.

Also in East Los Gatos, the old tank house, guest house, and remodeled barn are all that remain of Colonel James Parker's ranch, now Hillbrook School at **16000 Marchmont**.

A favorite landmark among the eucalyptus trees on the hill is the home at **17940 Saratoga-Los Gatos Road**. Built by the Mitchells in 1890, it has come to be known as the Clarence Hamsher house, after Los Gatos' long-time historian who lived there after 1922. Restoration is under way on the house, carriage house, and tank house.

This Queen Anne structure built by Cogswell in 1895 owes its long life at 115 North Santa Cruz to E. E. Place, who bought the house in 1920 for his furniture, funeral and ambulance business. Additions have been made, but the integrity of its style remains.

At the top of College Avenue, the Sacred Heart Novitiate and winery have been in operation since 1886 when the Jesuits bought the Harvey Wilcox property. The old winery building was destroyed by fire in 1934, but the stone aging cellars have survived, though enveloped by new structures. The covered walkways in the cloister area and the slaughter house (see photo) date from the earliest years. The only other pre-1920 buildings are the chapel, modernized dining room, and the Juniors' wing, built in 1915.

Considered the oldest structure in the mountains, the home built by John and Susan Schultheis on land they homesteaded in 1852, stands among redwood trees at **22849 Summit Road**. Schultheis, a skilled cabinetmaker, eventually covered over the rough, hand-hewn timbers with milled lumber. The large house on the property was built in 1880 by Volney Averill, who married Schultheis' daughter. A tank house, barn, and wood house are also in their original state.

This small frame structure and the house that overlooks it were witness to one of the mountain community's most interesting eras. William E. "Father" Riker arrived here in 1918 and founded a religious colony called Holy City. Over the years, a growing number of residents followed Riker's philosophy which he called the "Perfect Christian Divine Way." Riker lived in the house on this property (purchased from two sisters) located across from the post office on the **Old Santa Cruz Highway**. The decaying structures nearby were built during the 1920's and 1930's, using lumber from dismantled structures in San Francisco.

Sisters of Presentation College occupy the former Montezuma School for Boys (1911–1955) on **Bear Creek Road**. With very few additions, the Sisters adapted the pueblo-like structures, built by E. A. Rogers soon after the Boys School was founded. Despite a fire that destroyed the dining room in 1953, several original structures remain. In addition to simulations of pueblo forms, one building incorporates Mission Revival details and a modern addition. Another building is built of redwood with tree pole exterior supports; and still another is an orientalized frame bungalow that was brought from a nearby ranch and moved "over the vineyard" to be used as an administration center. Several other frame bungalows moved at the same time are still in use.

Nearby on **Bear Creek Road** stand the scattered structures from the former Alma College. Recent fires have left only the brick and concrete foundations of the grand old mansion built by James Flood in 1894, but other buildings remain. Now a private school, the estate has had several owners since Colonel S. H. Knowles, a former San Francisco Vigilante, developed the property in the 1880's. Flood, the "Bonanza King," sold it in 1906 to Dr. H. L. Tevis who maintained it until his death. The 970 acres were sold by his heirs in 1934 to the Jesuits for a School of Theology. Alma College remained here until 1967.

Campbell

Modest bungalows from the early days of Benjamin Campbell's subdivision still dot the downtown streets in a radius of five blocks around Campbell Avenue. The original J. C. Ainsley home from the 1890's is now at **112 North Second**, having been moved in three parts from its original site at Harrison and the railroad tracks, where Ainsley built his cannery in 1892. The original site is now marked by large walnut trees. The Ralph Hyde home at **227 East Alice** was built in 1917 on the old fruit drying yard, which was subdivided when the operation switched to canning.

This home at 91 South 2nd is Campbell's most historic, having been built by James Henry Campbell, Benjamin's son, in the 1880's.

Campbell's third banking institution, the Mercantile-Trust building now the Gaslight Theatre at **400 East Campbell Avenue**, is a startling concrete-and-marble edifice on an uncharacteristically small scale. The interior has marble wainscoting and the original black marble floors beneath the wood floor, which was installed when it was converted to a theatre in the 1930's.

An old ranch located along the creek bed, before it became Dry Creek Road, belonged to D. H. Leigh, for whom the avenue is named. The ranch house he bought in 1874 from John Guerraz survives, along with the old barn, amid new houses at **140 Peter Drive** and is believed to date to 1850. The owner added a picket fence and windmill from her family ranch in Gilroy. The large two-story Bert T. Kirk house built in 1899 stands on **Maykirk Road at Dry Creek**.

At 365 East Campbell, this structure was the first Bank of Campbell and at the time it was built in 1895, the only brick structure among frame buildings. Later owned by Guy Farley, it has come to be known as the Farley Building.

An unusual house for Campbell is this craftsmanly shingled residence with a Palladian window. Built by Eliphalet and Ida Price about 1902, it stands in its original condition at 1902 Dry Creek Road and is still occupied by the Price family.

" . . . I saw the valley, not as now only partially tamed and reveling in
the wild magnificence of nature, but from river bed to mountain
summit, humming with human life."

Bayard Taylor 1859

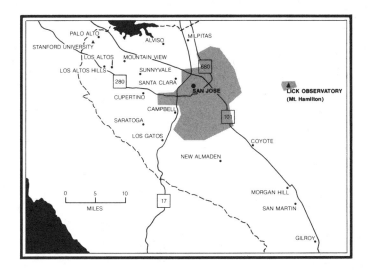

San Jose

It has taken nearly two hundred years for San Jose to fulfill its promising beginning as California's first pueblo.

In November 1777, 15 soldiers and settlers with their families were chosen from the presidios at San Francisco and Monterey to found Peublo San Jose de Guadalupe. Ten of the men had been with Anza's hardy band of pioneers when they founded Mission San Francisco just a year earlier. The rewards offered the new *pobladores* were generous. In addition to a house lot and two garden plots, they were offered 10 pesos a month plus army rations, horses, cattle, and agricultural supplies.

San Jose was the first of only three purely civilian colonies officially established in Spanish Alta California. It was followed by Los Angeles in 1781 and Branciforte (now part of Santa Cruz) in 1797. These pueblos were to serve as food production centers for the missions and presidios, long established tools of Spanish colonization.

Despite its location in the heart of a fertile valley the town was apparently of little influence, dominated as it was by the Presidio and port at San Francisco and the heavily populated and successful agricultural community that developed at nearby Mission Santa Clara. Still, it was a favorite place for retired soldiers from the garrisons at San Francisco and Monterey. Its attractions included a good climate and independence from the watchful eye of the padres and presidio officers.

By 1841 the pueblo's original population of 68 had grown to 300. Josiah Belden, a New Englander who came from Missouri with the first overland immigration party to California, passed through San Jose that year and described it as a small village with a few adobe and palizada (logs and earth) houses. The mode of life was very simple and conditions generally appeared

San Jose's Market Street and Santa Clara Street intersection, viewed in 1858 from the roof of the old City Hall looking south.

to him as primitive. Coyotes, he reported, howled nightly all about the outskirts of town.

At the outbreak of the Mexican War in 1846 the pueblo of San Jose had become a place of some promise, boasting a public house and three or four small stores and shops. Excitement ran high that July when dashing Captain Thomas Fallon rode into town with his gang of California volunteers, "took the *Juzgado*" (jailhouse), and raised the American flag. Many overland pioneer families of the early 1840's had settled in and around San Jose; it lay on the final leg of an immigrant trail from Sutter's Fort to San Francisco, which was then hardly more than a vague destination to the landlocked overland settlers who were looking for farm land. They found it in the fertile Valley of San Jose (as the vale was often called in those days) and these substantial people soon transformed the little pueblo into "The Garden City"

of California. San Jose's heyday came in December of 1849 when as the first state capital it hosted the original California legislative body. Land speculation ran wild and lots that cost the owners $10,000 were sold years later for less than a fourth of that amount.

After the gold rush, San Francisco became the economic and cultural center of the area. San Jose was a place of "sunshine, fruit and flowers" and was called the "loveliest inland city of California." Miraculously dozens of grand old Victorian-age houses have survived the rampant destruction of San Jose's once garden-like avenues and estates. In its bid to join in California's phenomenal postwar growth the old pueblo nearly lost sight of its heritage as the first civil settlement in the state. However, in 1972 San Jose's stately 1868 courthouse was refurbished in an overdue burst of civic pride and interest in its rich past. Plans are now underway to preserve and restore the historic Peralta Adobe, the last remnant of the old pueblo.

The Luis Peralta Adobe*

184 Saint John Street

The Peralta adobe is all that remains of the many adobe houses built around the Market Plaza of Pueblo San Jose, California's first civil settlement founded in 1777.

Don Luis Maria Peralta—soldier, Indian fighter, and grantee of one of the largest ranchos in California—was a legendary character in the valley's early days.
great disrepair, the sole survivor of more than a hundred that in the 1800's dotted the Pueblo San Jose de Guadalupe from today's Julian Street along the Market Plaza south to the vicinity of San Salvador Street.

His father, Corporal Gabriel Peralta, brought his wife and four children to California with the Anza expedition. The Peraltas were among the fifteen families listed in the first *padron* of San Jose in 1778. Luis was 18 when they helped establish the original pueblo which stood near the present County Civic Center a mile north of the old plaza.

As was traditional, Luis enlisted in the service of the King of Spain when he reached the age of 21. After his marriage to Maria Loreto Alviso in 1784, he transferred from Monterey to the San Francisco Company serving with the Escolta (guards) at Mission Santa Clara, Mission San Jose, and as corporal of the guard at the founding of Mission Santa Cruz.

In the early 1880's Sergeant Peralta commanded several expeditions against insurgent Indians. In 1805 following a bloody attack on the priest and major-domo at Mission San Jose, he led the full garrison from the fort at San Fran-cisco into the San Joaquin Valley in pursuit of the Indians. The troops, uniformed in multi-layered leather-jacket armor and deerskin shields, successfully surprised the Indians in their village, killing several and taking the rest prisoners. Peralta was credited with bringing peace at last to the troubled mission. The able sergeant was honored by appointment as *comisionado* in charge of Pueblo San Jose in 1807, the highest military and civil official, a position he was to hold until 1822 when the office ceased with Mexico's independence from Spanish authority.

Three years before taking over as *comisionado* Luis had been given two parcels of land by Jose Rosales, a son of one of the original pueblo settlers. Apparently the soldier-settler families (such as the Peraltas) were not granted any *suertes* as the farm lots were called.

---

* State Registered Landmark #866

134

Of the 15 pueblo founders only nine were distributed lots. A careful study of the list of original settlers shows that only those not on the army rosters received pueblo lands.

The 1804 deed conveying the land from Rosales to Luis Peralta is most interesting. Noting that he is the last surviving member of his family (excepting his little nephews), Jose Rosales went into a long explanation. He assured the powers-that-be that his widower brother-in-law agreed with his intention to transfer two of his *suertes* (he seemed to have a total of six—four were promised to his nephews) to "his" sergeant, Luis Peralta, "if the Governor will let me." He mentioned that in the year past he had loaned said two *suertes* to his "Maestro," the retired soldier Gabriel Peralta (Luis' father), and that he would like the land transferred at once, if possible. He signed on April 7, 1804 at Pueblo San Jose. According to the *comisionado*, at that time Macario Castro, Governor Arillaga in Loreto and "Senor Capitan" Jose Arguello at Presidio San Francisco both agreed to the

transfer and Luis took possession of the *suertes*. His extensive pear orchard was located on the west side of his land, between today's San Pedro Street and the Guadalupe River.

Recently a map of the pueblo dating from 1820 has come to light. The first of a row of houses shown on the map is marked "Casa de Manuel Gonzales Despues de Sargente Peralta."* This indication that the Peralta adobe may have belonged to Manuel Gonzales, an Apache Indian who was one of the original settlers of Pueblo San Jose and who died in 1804, should be considered as possibly uncovering the true date of the adobe. If it did indeed belong to Gonzales then the structure may date back to the 1790's when the pueblo was moved to higher ground due to flooding at the first pueblo site. However, no deed of transfer from Gonzales to Peralta has been located.

During his final years as *comisionado*, Peralta received the magnificent East Bay Rancho San Antonio patented by the United States for 43,473 acres, the first grant in the frontier land north of Mission San Jose. His four sons occupied the rancho; the aging Don Luis preferred to live at his house in San Jose. In time he became the patriarch of the pueblo. Two of his daughters, Josefa and Guadalupe, remained with him there, where he died in 1851. In conjunction with the Peralta Adobe Restoration Committee the Junior League of San Jose has pledged funds to establish an educational program and a permanent history display to be mounted in the plaza fronting the restored adobe.

---

* Information courtesy of Frances Fox.

The Roberto-Sunol adobe on Lincoln Avenue, Willow Glen area of San Jose.

The Roberto–Sunol Adobe

770 Lincoln Avenue

Out on Lincoln Avenue in the midst of what was once Mission Santa Clara's swine range, on Rancho Los Coches (the pigs), sits a romantic old house. A faded emblem over its wooden gate reads "Laura Ville," a reminder of the days when it was the home of Don Antonio Sunol, a French speaking Spaniard who had served as a cadet in the French navy and had come to live in California in 1818.

Described as short, dapper, rosy-cheeked, he appeared more like a French pastry chef (dressed in a white cap and apron) than the Alcalde of Pueblo San Jose to Lt. Charles Wilkes of the U. S. Naval exploring expedition, when Wilkes visited San Jose in 1841. A gregarious man who was involved in a dozen enterprises, Sunol made a fortune and held on to it, unlike his more easy going Californio neighbors. He married Maria Dolores Bernal and was said to have been the first man to try to work his brother-in-law Jose Reyes Berryesa's mine in New Almaden for silver (without success).* Don Antonio was postmaster and also kept a grog shop in San Jose.

Los Coches is especially interesting since it was one of the few ranchos in California granted to and occupied by an Indian. The Christianized Indian grantee, Roberto Balermino, in fact built part of the existing house. The ground floor is made up of two separate

---

* See Berreyesa Adobe, Chapter 5, Santa Clara, and Chapter 9, New Almaden.

Don Antonio Sunol was not only San Jose's first postmaster but also kept a popular grog shop in pueblo days.

After a successful venture in the gold fields, Sunol and his son-in-law Pedro Sainsevain returned to Rancho Los Coches. Here, Pedro, who had worked for his uncle (the renowned southern California viniculturist Jean Louis Vignes), planted some of the earliest grapevines in the Santa Clara Valley. In spite of problems with squatters, Don Antonio entertained lavishly at his adobe during California's first legislative session in 1849–50. The next few years, however, were unhappy ones for the Sunols and their kinsmen; five cousins of Sunol's wife's family were murdered, including their eldest son Jose Antonio Sunol.

Don Antonio sold the house and surrounding vineyard in 1853 to Captain Stefano Splivalo, an Italian sea captain. It was Captain Splivalo who encased the 18-inch thick walls in wood and added a full second story frame addition and balcony, reminiscent of Monterey-style houses. The frosted glass door is said to have been brought round the Horn by Captain Splivalo, as were the shingled shutters covering the 7-foot windows. The captain may have brought his taste for New England touches from the East coast ports in his seafaring days.

The Splivalo family lived in the house for nearly 40 years. After the Captain died in 1891 the house passed through several hands. The last resident owner, Miss Elayne Basuini had lived in the place since she was a child. Following her death and probate settlement, it was purchased for use as an office by a man fortunately sympathetic to the preservation of the historic Roberto-Sunol Adobe.

structures. One is a small one-room adobe built by Roberto, who lived there with his family from 1836 until 1847 when he transferred title of the rancho to Sunol in payment of a $500 debt. The second structure of kiln-fired adobe brick was built adjoining the Indian's house probably in 1847 when Don Antonio took over the rancho.

Captain Thomas Fallon's House

175 Saint John Street

If one looks carefully at the present facade of the Italian Cellar Restaurant there is evidence of the formal beauty of this large Italianate home, built in 1859 by "Captain" Thomas Fallon just across the road from the Peralta Adobe.

Thomas Fallon had all the makings of a folk hero—a fine looking man with courtly manners and a ready Irish wit; his story has found a place in the legends of the Mexican War in California. Born in Ireland in 1824, he was sent to Canada as a boy and bound out as an apprentice in the saddler's trade. His love of adventure spurred him to take his chances in the American West. At 18 he headed for Texas and the following year in the company of some fellow romantics embarked on the "novel enterprise" of marching to the Pacific coast, arriving in the spring of 1844.

He settled in Santa Cruz and became well known for his craftsmanship in making the favorite Mexican saddle tree. When word of the Bear Flag Revolt reached Fallon and his friends in Santa Cruz in June of 1846, they simply decided, in Fallon's words, "to raise a party and go help them." The self-styled captain apparently had little trouble raising a party of 20 or so men. They crossed the Santa Cruz mountains and camped near San Jose. Fallon was considered a man of "courage and discretion," which he soon proved by judiciously dodging Colonel Jose Castro and his force of Californio soldiers.

After the end of the Mexican War Fallon returned to Santa Cruz where

Captain Thomas Fallon who raised the American flag over San Jose in 1846.

in 1848 he married Carmelita Lodge, beautiful half Irish, half Spanish daughter of one of the area's largest landowners. Everything literally turned to gold that year for Thomas. At Big Bar in the goldfields he made a fortune in a few months, and back in Santa Cruz built a large frame building facing Mission Plaza; it was a combination residence, store, and hotel. In 1850 Carmelita received one ninth of her mother Martina Castro's 34,000-acre Rancho Soquel. Thomas sold their house to newly formed Santa Cruz County for

Thomas Fallon's house as it appears in Thompson and West's historical atlas of 1876. The grounds of the house extended to San Pedro Street.

use as the county courthouse and the Fallons packed up and left to live in Texas.

After the tragic death of three of their children there, in 1854 they returned to California and Thomas began to buy up acres of land in San Jose. In 1859 while serving as mayor of San Jose, Fallon built this house, one of the town's finest residences. The estate then extended to the corner of San Pedro and Saint John Streets and was fronted by formal gardens. But all was not well with the Fallon household. In spite of reports that he was never actually untrue to Carmelita, before long she divorced him and moved back to Santa Cruz. Fallon remarried in 1875. For awhile Annie, the youngest of his three daughters remained living in San Jose with him and his second wife.

In 1882, Thomas Fallon divorced her, closed the San Jose house and moved to San Francisco's Lick House. Even at his death in 1885, age 60, the old Fallon charm was at work; an unsettled breach of promise suit against him was pending trial. The litigation over his considerable fortune continued into the 1920's.

The lovely old house with its tree-filled grounds sat empty for several years until the 1890's when a kindergarten moved in for a time. In 1894 it was taken over as a boarding house. Catering to San Jose's growing Italian population, it became L'Italia Hotel, and eventually The Italian Cellar, a popular San Jose restaurant.

The Murphy Building

36 South Market Street

The Murphy Building well represents the civil and social history of Santa Clara County during its early days. Although its facade is covered by a layer of stucco, the structure still retains many original features as well as its basic architectural integrity. It has been recognized as a fine example of pre or early Civil War Era commercial building which once stood in so many northern California towns.

Rescued more than two years ago within days of its proposed demolition to make way for a parking lot, the landmark building stands as the result of a citizen's challenge to its destruction. A landmark case in historic preservation followed, attacking the sufficiency of the Negative (no-effect) Environmental Impact Report which would have allowed the razing of the 113-year-old former county courthouse. It was found to be of sufficient historical and architectural significance to be listed in the prestigious *National Register of Historic Places* in April 1975. Of the building the keeper of the National Register William J. Murtagh had this to say:

> When the professional staff of the National Register reviewed the nomination for the Murphy Building and other information that was submitted, the building was found to be clearly eligible for listing in the National Register and worthy of preservation for its significance in the history of San Jose and Santa Clara County. Constructed as a multipurpose commercial building, and used for a

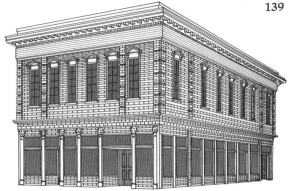

The Murphy building as it appeared in the 19th century when it was the county courthouse.

courthouse and post office early in its history, the Murphy Building is a rare surviving example of such mid-nineteenth-century structures in California. Early photographs also indicate that the building was conceived as a substantial and somewhat pretentious addition to San Jose in the 1860's. The attention to architectural detail—pedimented windows, ornamented window surrounds, the elegant restrained cornice, and correct proportions—separated the building from its neighbors. Though some of these elements are missing today, the basic proportions and cornice remain, and contemporary photographic documentation would permit an accurate restoration of the lost details.

Martin Murphy Junior.

With the destruction in 1961 of Martin Murphy's beautiful home in Sunnyvale—said to have been brought around the Horn in 1849—little if anything other than San Jose's Murphy Building remains to memorialize Martin Murphy, Jr., or the pioneer generation of his family.

In 1850 Martin Murphy, Jr., eldest son of the large clan headed by his father Martin Murphy, settled on the Rancho Pastoria de las Borregas establishing the ranch that would some day become the site of Sunnyvale* (but was for years called Murphy's Station). Murphy Junior was a shrewd businessman and purchased several strategic parcels in San Jose. One of the first of these was in Block 1, Range 1 North of the original 1847 survey of the then Pueblo of San Jose. This block, where the Murphy Building stands, was the center of the civic and commercial life of San Jose and the county.

When in 1862 Martin Murphy undertook the construction of the building, the county court sessions were being held in the San Jose City Hall located a block away from the Murphy Building on Market Street. On November 8, 1862 Murphy entered into a lease with the Board of Supervisors. The upper story of his brick building was in the process of completion and was fitted out especially for use as the "county Court of Record." It is the opinion of the Preservation Chairman of the Coast Counties Chapter of the AIA that the structure was expressly designed for court use and that it was designed by a professional architect. It is of the modified 16th century Italian style appropriate to its period and identical to the State Supreme Court building in Sacramento currently being restored. The upstairs court location is true also to its time and style. The large 63-by-40-foot courtroom was reached by a relatively wide staircase leading from the street to the anteroom; two rooms used as jury rooms are off this

---

* See Chapter 2, Mountain View—Sunnyvale

anteroom. Double doors which may be original open into the former courtroom which has an extremely high ceiling and an original roll cornice. The original tall narrow windows are there and the courtroom is nearly as it was except for the later addition of light weight wooden partitions that divided the room into several smaller rooms. (In the last several decades the building has been used for many purposes—a gambling hall, supposedly a bordello. These partitions date from those days and could easily be removed revealing the original courtroom.)

Court sessions were held here from January 1863 to January 1868 when they were moved into the just completed "new" courthouse.* During this five-year period the Civil War was underway and much of the local debate over the fate of the Union took place here in this frontier courthouse. Here the outstanding figures of Santa Clara County's history, including pioneer judges, attorneys, and county officials worked and argued the course of the county's future. The Murphy Building holds the spirit of these men and many more from its rich past when it served not only as the county courthouse but also as the Third District Court of the State of California. Later, in 1868, it was the U. S. Post Office.

161 North First Street (Off St. James Park)

Santa Clara County has long been justly proud of its handsome Neo-Classical courthouse, restored and rededicated in 1973 after 105 years of service. The handsome structure was designed on the Roman-Corinthian order by pioneer California architect, Levi Goodrich. The excellent restoration was designed by John C. Worsley, Chief of the California Department of Architecture, who also supervised the conscientious refurbishing.

No longer does the "strong-ribbed and gracefully-curved dome" rise above the spacious building as it did when it was completed in 1868 and declared "the finest courthouse in the state." According to Harold Kirker it was the last important county building constructed in California before the completion of the transcontinental railroad. The 50-foot dome which originally topped the courthouse was marked by a series of 11 elliptical windows. Early San Jose residents recall climbing the 172 steps within the dome's lofty height to reach an iron-railed observation deck 115 feet above the city. In May of 1931 a disastrous fire gutted much of the building. The lofty dome as well as the strong, simple pediment that surmounted the classical, columned portico was not replaced when the building was rebuilt in 1932. Instead, a third story was added.

---

* See The Old County Courthouse, this chapter.

The old Santa Clara County Courthouse designed in 1866 by Levi Goodrich and restored in 1973 by John C. Worsley A.I.A.

The original sturdy brick outer walls remained in perfect condition, having survived the 1906 earthquake as well as the 1931 fire—a testimonial to the ability of architect Levi Goodrich. Son of a New York architect, Goodrich, who was also an accomplished engraver, is also credited with designing the original University of the Pacific buildings, Notre Dame Convent, and the first State Normal School, all at San Jose, plus the county courthouses in Monterey and San Diego.

No sooner had Goodrich's impressive Santa Clara County edifice been completed in 1868 (at a cost of over $173,000) than the board of supervisors revived earlier efforts to persuade the state legislature to reinstate San Jose as the state capital. Use of the new courthouse was offered free of charge until such time as a new state capitol building could be erected. The members of the legislature were invited to inspect the magnificent premises and the city of San Jose as a suitable seat of state government. However, construction was well underway on the present capitol building in Sacramento (begun in 1861) and the legislature declined the offer.

The fine old courthouse, which nature chose not to destroy through the years, was very nearly demolished by the county government in 1965 when it was recommended that the building be razed along with its longtime neighbor, the 1905 Hall of Records, site of the contemporary brick Superior Court Building completed in 1966. The courthouse's fate was uncertain for the next several years until Judge Marshall S. Hall and other members of the county's 24-man superior court bench recognized the economic benefits as well as the historical value of remodelling the structurally sound building to provide badly needed additional courtrooms.

In the course of preparing the venerable building for the nearly one-million-dollar remodelling job in 1972, workmen discovered a long forgotten vault sealed behind a solid brick wall in the cellar and filled with a treasure trove of old documents. Among the tax rolls and ledgers, they found some unique Mexican-era *disenos*, hand drawn boundary maps required by Mexican authorities of citizens petitioning for the grant of a rancho in pre-American California. Many of the documents were partially burned and watersoaked and had obviously survived the 1931 fire.

The abandoned vault had heavy steel doors and grim, barred windows curiously set at ground level in the four-foot thick brick walls. The room appeared to be a former cell block for prisoners, perhaps dating from before the erection of the old county jail, which once stood to the rear of the courthouse. But it seems more likely to have been used in early days as the county sheriff's stable. A stable of horses was kept there for the sheriff and his deputies to ride out as a posse in pursuit of justice.

A throng of citizens turned out for the refurbished courthouse's dedication ceremonies on April 23, 1973—the third in its history. Admirers viewed the elegantly restored marble-floored halls lit by newly designed period style chandeliers. The original two courtrooms (increased in 1879 to three) have been divided into a total of five courts, decorated in brilliant primary colors. The largest and grandest "Green Court" occupies the original 1868 main courtroom.

The Lick Observatory At Mount Hamilton

Twenty-six Miles Up Mt. Hamilton Road

It is said that San Francisco's legendary William Ralston, President of the Bank of California and creator of the Palace Hotel, suggested the great acts of philanthropy adopted by the penurious James Lick. Ailing, perhaps fearful of death, Lick may have realized he could not take his millions with him.

Ralston himself may have been responsible for the final noble tribute accorded James Lick when he was at last buried beneath the great pier of what was then the world's largest telescope, high atop 4,029-foot Mount Hamilton, "a tomb such as no old-world monarch could have imagined."

At a meeting of the California Academy of Sciences on October 23, 1873, James Lick's intention to build an observatory was announced by Academy President George Davidson of the Coast Geodetic Survey. The location was to be left to Mr. Lick's discretion. He was said to be inclined toward a site near Lake Tahoe. When this proved impractical, a place on Mount Saint Helena was temporarily considered, but on the advice of his confidential agent, Thomas E. Fraser, Mount Hamilton was chosen, supposedly because of the City of San Jose's eloquent expressions of appreciation for Lick's gift of $25,000 for the construction of an orphan asylum. One suspects Lick Estate Trustee B. D. Murphy, son of county pioneer Martin

Murphy, Jr., and onetime Mayor of San Jose, was largely responsible for the Santa Clara County site being chosen. James Lick addressed the Santa Clara County Board of Supervisors in September 1875, offering to locate his proposed observatory on Mount Hamilton if the county would build a first-class road to the summit. The following month a preliminary survey was ordered, and 15 months later, after much ado and considerable difficulty with contractors, the Mount Hamilton Road (or Lick Avenue as it was occasionally called) was completed at a cost of $73,458.

James Lick died in 1876 having executed his final trust deed for $700,000 to purchase the initial 1900 acres of land and to construct the telescope ("superior to and more powerful than any yet made") and a "suitable observatory connected therewith." It was designated The Lick Astronomical Department of the University of California.

On January 9, 1887, when the observatory was nearly completed, James Lick's casket was moved from Lone Mountain Cemetery in San Francisco to San Jose, where, accompanied by a procession of officials, it was taken atop the mountain and placed with due pomp in a tomb prepared in the foundation of the column supporting the great 36-inch telescope, which had just reached the facility several days earlier.

The fortress-like main observatory building, which still stands, was begun in 1881, the first construction being the tower holding the 12-inch lens, which was completed by 1882. The adjoining body of the structure connecting the two domes was constructed under the

A series of observatories have been constructed along the summit ridge of Mt. Hamilton. In the center of the picture is the one James Lick made possible and which was begun in 1881.

supervision of Thomas Fraser. On June 15, 1886, the cornerstone was laid for the big dome to hold the 36-inch lens, which had been cast in France and made true by Alvan G. Clark and Sons of Massachusetts in 1885 after an earlier casting had cracked in packing. The general layout of the building seems to have been a joint effort by Professor Simon Newcomb of the Naval Observatory in Washington, D. C. (who had acted as consultant to the project off and one since 1874) and West Point graduate Professor Edward S. Holden, also an astronomer with the Navy. Holden

served as advisor to the observatory trustees from 1881 to 1885, when he became temporary president of the University of California. A rough sketch diagramming the observatory facility is included in correspondence between Newcomb and Holden dating from 1879. The actual plans were done by S. Edwards Todd, Jr. a Washington, D. C., architect.

146   On June 1, 1888 the entire facility was completed and officially turned over to the University of California by the Lick Trustees. Professor Holden had taken up residence as director at Mount Hamilton in May, having resigned as president of the university. The only other major structure on the mountain at that time was the "old dormitory" for graduate students in astronomy, which included a spacious apartment where Holden lived. An earthquake in 1911 caused considerable damage to that building and it was replaced by the large dormitory building which stands today, designed in 1913 by John Galen Howard, the head of the Department of Architecture at the University of California.

Two other buildings still stand on Mt. Hamilton from the famous observatory's first years. Still there is Professor Barnard's brick residence built in 1894 by architect G. W. Page of San Jose, and Professor William W. Campbell's home, also built by architect Page in 1894 and remodelled in 1923 to serve as the director's residence.

The Winchester House*

525 South Winchester Boulevard

It wasn't until Sarah Winchester died at the age of 85 in September 1922 that work on her bizarre, multi-gabled 160-room house finally stopped. The owners of the fantastic Eastlake-shingle-Queen Anne tourist attraction have cashed in on its "mystery" status through the years, but the remarkable house on which the widow of the heir to the Winchester Repeating Arms Company spent an estimated five million dollars is truly a marvel of craftsmanship. Recently it was granted State Landmark status as a unique embodiment of elaborate architectural details no longer possible to reproduce in any one structure. The abundance of timber within close proximity to San Jose allowed Mrs. Winchester's imagination free reign to try out what was evidently her consuming interest in architectural innovation.

In June of 1886 Sarah Pardee Winchester paid J. H. Hamm $12,570 in gold coin for nearly 45 acres of land on the "Santa Cruz-Santa Clara Road" (today's Winchester Boulevard). The parcel included a house of 8 or 9 rooms reported to still be under construction when she purchased it. When the 49-year-old widow came to the Santa Clara Valley from New Haven, Connecticut, her sister Isabelle Pardee Merriman and family came with her.** The Merriman's daughter Marian had been living with

---

* State Registered Landmark #868

** See the Merriman-Winchester Ranch, Chapter 3, Los Altos.

The unbelievable array of towers, turrets, spires and arches that make up the Winchester House.

her Aunt Sarah for many years prior to the family's coming to California. The lonely Mrs. Winchester, who had originally planned to bring her husband out to California for his health (and whose only child had died some years earlier) was not yet fabulously rich. When her husband William Wirt Winchester died in 1881 of tuberculosis, she received less than 10% of the company stock. It wasn't until 1904 that she inherited a reported 20 million dollars, the bulk of the Winchester family shares in the company.

Most of the outlandishly extravagant additions seem to date from after this time. Neither an 1895 nor 1901 account of the house (or photographs from these dates) display anything unusual about the house, other than its being singled out as a residence of some note. Also by 1904 Mrs. Winchester had purchased and was living in a "fine residence" in Menlo Park on six acres of land, according to an item in the *Palo Alto Times*

Sarah Pardee Winchester in what is said to be the only known picture ever taken of her.

(October 1903). She probably then felt free, with or without alleged spiritual guidance, to try any experiments in architectural design to her heart's content.

The tiny intelligent woman had been a generous philanthropist throughout her life, as were her sister Isabelle Merriman and her neice Marian Merriman (later Mrs. Frederick Marriott), who inherited a large sum of money from her aunt Sarah's estate as well as her fabulous house. The money was in a life estate which on Marian's death went to a tuberculosis hospital established in 1911 by Sarah Winchester as a memorial to her husband.

Shortly after Mrs. Winchester's death in 1922 the house was sold and then opened to the public as the Winchester Mystery House. It was an instant success. An estimated million people have viewed Sarah Winchester's fabulous structure covering six acres with its array of roofs, towers, and spires. There are rooms with gold plated fixtures, and exquisite doors and windows of stained Tiffany glass set in silver designs—a thousand things of beauty to see, as well as practical household innovations years ahead of their time.

Supplement

San Jose

San Jose, the "Heart of Santa Clara Valley," has remained the concentrated vital center of a thriving agricultural valley for much of its 200 years. Its phenomenal post-1940's growth accounts for most of what has been destroyed or endangered of the city's fragile heritage. But still a great deal remains—often in unexpected places. In fact, San Jose is unique in the Bay Area for the variety of its architectural styles and the number of fine examples still standing today. The downtown area has several sections well suited for "historic district" designation, most notably St. James Square, which is surrounded by noteworthy structures. In addition to the Courthouse, Trinity Church, and the Sainte Claire Club, other pre-1920 structures include on **North 3rd**, the unique Unitarian Church, an interesting combination of styles built in 1891 by G. W. Page; the Eagles Club next door with its Classical Revival facade; and at **43 East St. James**, the domed Christian Science Church, used from 1905–46 now serving as a theater.

In the historic old business district, across from the Murphy Building at **Market and Post**, the red brick building labeled Metropole Hotel was built in 1890 as the Alcantara Building. On an historical corner, this was the site of the old Pueblo's *juzgado* of 1798, where the Bear Flag was raised in 1846, declaring American dominance over the territory, then ruled by Mexico. For nearly a century, the old Home Union building next door, across Post Street, stood until demolished in 1975.

The oldest church structure in San Jose, the Victorian Gothic redwood Trinity Episcopal Church on North 2nd at St. John, was built in 1863. Cut in half and pulled apart by horse teams in 1876, it was rebuilt in the form of a cross and features fine interior carpentry. Additions in 1884 included the church rooms, the tower and spire, which house what are called "the oldest chimes in the west."

A mixture of architectural ideas (designed by A. Page Brown who also designed the San Francisco Ferry Building), the Sainte Claire Club at 65 East St. James was built in 1894 as a private men's club by James D. Phelan, United States Senator from 1915–21.

Recently called "the outstanding example of Mission Revival architecture in the Bay Area," by the authors of the AIA guide to Northern California, the 1911 First Methodist Church dominates the intersection of East Santa Clara and North 5th.

The Richardson Romanesque "Old Post Office," at
Market and San Fernando, *was built of sandstone
blocks in 1892 by Willoughby Edbrooke. It has twice
re-adapted to the community's changing needs, becoming
the city library in 1937 and the art museum in 1971.*

*Among a few relics from San Jose's oldest business district, this structure, built during the 1860's at 65 Post
Street, was known as Sullivan's Saloon at the turn of the
century. Its neighbor across Lightstone Alley was possibly
built earlier.*

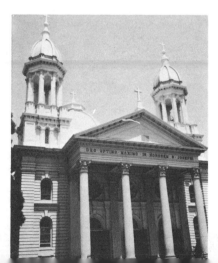

Above the street level, the fine old structures
along **South First Street** can still be appreciated. Notable are : **52 South First**, which
served as a Masonic Hall from 1870–83; and
the Letitia Building at **66-72 South First**,
designed by Jacob Lenzen for C. T. Ryland
in 1890 and named for Ryland's wife who
was the daughter of Peter Burnett, first Governor of the State of California. The adjacent Ryland Block was added in 1892 and
fills the rest of the block to East San Fernando.

In the **200 block on South First** are: the
old Montgomery Hotel, designed in 1911 by
William Curtis for T. S. Montgomery, prominent builder of the post-earthquake era;
and the old Hippodrome vaudeville house
from 1918—later a movie theatre after extensive remodeling. The oldest theatre still
in business in San Jose is at **64 South Second**, now called the "Jose."

Rebuilt after the 1906 earthquake, the
building at the corner of **2nd and East San
Fernando** housed L. Lion and Sons furniture
store from 1908–64.

The last remnant of the "railroad district"—the area around the old depot on
Basset Street—is the Fox Saloon, built in
1873 and still standing at **448 North San
Pedro.** The simple false-front frame structure is being restored by its new owner.

Not far away at **93 North Devine**, the
home of G. W. Lowery has stood since the
1860's. No doubt saved by its adaptive use
as a funeral chapel, it was remodeled and
pillars added to the facade after 1909.

The old San Jose Normal School has
existed here since moving from San Francisco in 1870. The oldest structures on the
campus are the Mission Revival Tower and
auditorium. The tower was built in 1911 and
the 1919 auditorium was named for President Morris E. Dailey on **South 7th Street**.

*St. Joseph's Catholic Church at Market and San Fernando, was designed by Brian Clinch and built in 1877
on the site of the original 1803 adobe church. Also notable
are the 1891 St. Mary's German Catholic Church at 565
South Second and the Portuguese Church of the Five
Wounds, at 1375 East Santa Clara, built in 1916.*

Kelley Park on **Senter Road at Story** was originally the Archer-Kelley estate. In addition to a zoo, children's park, Japanese Gardens, and community center, the park has a large area devoted to the San Jose Historical Museum. The grounds include room for a replica park of downtown San Jose, part of which has been completed. The Print Shop and Dashaway Stables were recently reconstructed. The old Umbarger house and Dr. Warburton's Office were relocated here and will be set on foundations. When completed, the structures will combine museums and businesses and will help make San Jose's heritage live for future generations.

The old Jackson School at **2031 Story Road** has been much remodeled since 1865 and has served as a commercial hall for several years. The 1913 McKinley School remains at **1122 Fair Avenue** but is now used as a clubhouse.

At **2281 McKee Road** is the home of one of San Jose's great benefactors, William Overfelt. The neat, two-story frame house was built in 1865. The Overfelt family donated land for a city park and for Alexian Brothers Hospital.

The Wool farm house (1870's) at the end of **Quinn Road** stands adjacent to F. G. Wool Packing Company, second largest canning operation in California and the oldest family-owned fruit processing plant. Four generations of the Wool family have worked here since its founding in the 1890's.

The Cottle Ranch in Edenvale, south of San Jose, still stands at **5285 Snell Road**. The Italianate ranch house was built in the 1880's and sits amidst oak trees and outbuildings, surrounded by open fields—the way it has for nearly 100 years.

At 34 South First, this charming commercial structure in Frank Furness' vivacious manner of design was built in 1889 by twice-widowed Sarah Knox-Goodrich on property owned by her first husband, Dr. William Knox, and with sandstone from the quarry in Almaden Valley owned by her second husband, the architect Levi Goodrich. The intertwined initials K & G, as well as the date are there for all to read.

Built by the De Saisset family to commemorate the New Century, this Renaissance Revival commercial structure stands at the corner of East Santa Clara and South 2nd. Attached on East Santa Clara are two structures labeled IOOF, the corner building constructed in 1883. Used for many years as a meeting hall for the International Order of Odd Fellows, it is now a gymnasium.

Where Lenzen and Montgomery Streets meet the Southern Pacific railroad tracks, this "Roundhouse" has stored engines since 1906 when it was reconstructed following the earthquake. Originally much larger, it has been reduced to four stalls. The last balance turntable on Southern Pacific's line, located here, was built by American Bridge Company in 1906.

The Moir Building stands at the corner of North First and Devine and was built in the 1890's, originally housing the Staford Hotel and more recently the St. James Hotel.

Of particular historical note are : The carriage house built by Judge Samuel Lieb a century ago and later remodeled as a home, is all that remains of the former estate at **60 North Keeble**. The home and carriage house of General Henry Morris Naglee at **95 & 99 South 14th** were once part of a 140-acre estate. This was his second house and both structures, built by the former Civil War officer sometime after he settled on this property in 1865, are now converted to apartments.

The cottage at **432 South Eighth** was inhabited by poet Edwin Markham from 1869–89, during the time he wrote his popular poem, "The Man with the Hoe."

The large farm house and barns of J. H. M. Townsend remain in poor condition at **1585 Schallenberger Road**. Son of pioneer doctor John Townsend, J. H. M. built this house about 1873, eventually farming 300 acres at this site.

Originally built by the Ashworths in 1875, the house at **755 Story Road** was purchased by the Remillard family in 1890. Their brick factory, built adjacent, was demolished in 1974. Daughter Lillian Remillard-Dandini maintained this as a summer home until her death.

The present East San Jose branch of the public library at **1102 East Santa Clara Street** was built in 1907, using funds from the Andrew Carnegie Foundation. The town of East San Jose existed here from 1906 until it was absorbed into San Jose in 1911.

This 1895 laundry which bears its founder's name of Troy, is still a laundry facility at 722 Almaden Avenue.

Dozens of fine pre-1900 houses exist in the blocks surrounding downtown San Jose. Italianate mansions from the 1860's–1880's once dominated whole blocks. Others were designed as apartments or row houses in varying degrees of Italianate styling. Excellent twin houses were built in this period at **193–197 North 5th**; and at **156 East St. John** the Allen Apartments were a favorite landmark. Built in the 1870's, they suffered a disastrous fire in 1974.

Two good examples of this styling are at **620 and 792 South 3rd**. At **693 South 2nd** the home and carriage house of Dr. Breyfogle—who practiced medicine, established a Building & Loan Association, and served as mayor in 1886—can still be appreciated. Another house at **482 South 2nd** is presently occupied by the San Jose Art League.

Well-kept, interesting twin houses at **31–37 Julian**, which have been converted into shops and apartments, were built circa 1895 in the Queen Anne style.

San Jose's only Bernard Maybeck designed structure will soon be restored at 62 South 13th. Built for H. B. Gates in 1904, it was owned by the Paul Masson family from 1928–35 and until recently was a fraternity house.

At 1163 Martin is a representative work of architects Wolfe and Wolfe. A bungalow designed for Eugene Coe in 1910, it features "arts and crafts" windows. As part of Hanchett Residence Park, (bounded by Alameda, Hester, Park, and Race Streets), the area was developed by T. S. Montgomery in 1910–20, with landscape design by John McLaren. Martin Street has numerous bungalow variations. Other Wolfe and Wolfe designs are found at 1208 Martin, 1151 Sierra, and 1299 Yosemite. Another at 2662 Monterey Road near Umbarger, was built in 1915 and used as a speakeasy during Prohibition.

*A rare mansarded roof crowns the 1870's house at **483 South Sixth**. Also notable is the pecan tree in the front yard, apparently the only fertile one in Santa Clara Valley! Another "rare" but simpler mansarded house is at 408 South Third and is believed to date from the 1860's.*

Called the Rucker House, this 1890's Queen Anne-Eastlake mansion and carriage house can be seen at 418 South 3rd. Another fine example of this commonly used, and often misunderstood architectural style, can be found at 295 East San Fernando; but the ultimate would have to be the small but fascinating Victorian-age wonder at 530 Sixth Street. Notable for its unusual lines, the Queen Anne-style home at 155 East Empire was the wedding gift from John Auzerais to his son Louis in 1890.

Still an orchard and vineyard settlement southeast of San Jose, old "Evergreen" maintains traces of its heritage through the scattered structures that remain, despite the rapid encroachment of housing developments.

The familiar Cribari Winery property was once a 718-acre parcel of Rancho Yerba Buena owned by J. McCarty in the 1870's and sold to William Wehner in 1888. Wehner built his large home and winery here in 1889. The Cribari name was not attached to the property until 1945, after which it was developed into 1,000 acres of orchard and vineyards. The future of this property is uncertain, as it is now in the hands of developers, but it still exists on **Vilia Vista Road.**

The Hassler Ranch on **Silver Creek Road** was settled in 1853, the old house, stock barns, and wooden tank are now abandoned.

The Francis Smith house has seen five generations of the same family since its construction in 1874 at **388 San Felipe Road**, an extension of White Road. Nearby at **3395 White Road**, an old farm house has been reprieved by the Hulse family to operate as a small nursery—a fine example of adaptive use that preserves the character of a "nice old house."

A rarity for this or any neighborhood is the small house at 1048 West San Fernando with a Queen Anne tower squashed into a cross plan. Another house at 960 West Taylor features an unusual hexagonal tower.

While the residential section of San Jose called "Willow Glen" is characterized mostly by neat, post-1920 row bungalows, there are some outstanding large residences from the pre-1920 period, many handsomely set in groves of beautiful old trees. One such example is the Georgian-style house at **1550 Hicks Avenue**, home of Dr. Charles M. Richards, the original benefactor of the San Jose Symphony. Built after 1906, the house has a carriage house and maids' quarters at the rear.

South of Willow Glen, at the corner of **Union and Almaden Road**, near Los Gatos, is the "We and Our Neighbors Club," founded in the 1890's and still housed in the redwood structure built in 1910.

The David Greenawalt home at **14611 Almaden Expressway** was built magnificently in 1877, an Italianate-style structure with marble fireplaces and a 12-foot deep sandstone basement. It deteriorates slowly as the commercial centers surrounding it continue their encroachment.

A potential for preservation, the once magnificent Renaissance-Revival-style Edenvale estate of Congressman E. A. Hayes and his brother J. O. Hayes (former publishers of the San Jose *Mercury-Herald*) still stands at **200 Edenvale Avenue**. The 60-room house built in 1910 is hidden behind Frontier Village, which was built on the front garden acres along the Monterey Road.

The large Italianate-style home, set in beautifully manicured gardens at 1615 Dry Creek Road, was built by Theophilus Kirk in 1878. Originally part of a 1,000-acre farm purchased in 1853 by Kirk and his brother Socrates, the land was gradually sold to developers, but the house has remained in the family. Nearby at 1725 Dry Creek at Peregrino, the charming W. S. Goodenough home was built by Socrates Kirk's son-in-law in 1905.

The most obvious landmark in Old Willow Glen is the Victorian-age, Eclectic-style mansion known as the Maynard House. At 1151 Minnesota, it was built in 1898 of virgin redwood, sandstone and brick, and constructed with square nails. It features a tower surrounded by an enclosed walk, a round wooden door, and a stained glass window in the brick chimney!

"Near the head of the beautiful and fertile valley of San Jose and in the eastern spur of the coast range of mountains is the quicksilver mine of New Almaden."

Hutchings Illustrated California Magazine, *Vol. 1, 1856*

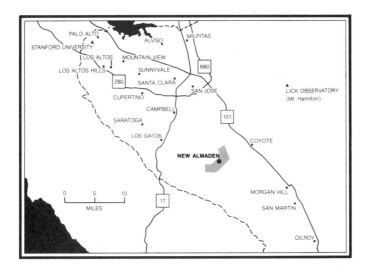

New Almaden

Nestled in a canyon 11 miles south of San Jose between the Pueblo Hills and the spurs of the Santa Cruz Mountains sits the tiny village of New Almaden, the once world famous quicksilver mining community that evolved on Jose Reyes Berreyesa's* Rancho San Vicente during the early 1850's.

When Captain Castillero of Mexico and his Californio partners gave control of their "Mine of Santa Clara" to the Barron–Forbes Company in 1846, they had barely begun development of the site along Alamitos Creek. Alexander Forbes, the majority stockholder in the new ownership came north from his mill and mercantile operation at Tepic, Mexico, in October of 1847, bringing a crew of Mexican workers to construct the initial facilities at the mine**, which Forbes renamed "New Almaden" after the fabulously rich quicksilver mine in Almaden, Spain.

In 1850, Henry Wager Halleck, a captain in the Army Corps of Engineers and secretary of state during the U. S. military government of California, was hired by Barron-Forbes to act as general manager of their New Almaden Mining Company. Halleck's knowledge of California land law was unsurpassed. Although still in the Army he had become a partner in the most successful San Francisco law firm of its time. While his partners pursued New Almaden's mining claim through the courts, Captain Halleck supervised construction of more efficient facilities at the Hacienda de Beneficio, the reduction headquarters, which lay at the base of the mine hills. Halleck, as general manager of the mine, was an inspired choice to guide the mine's initial development. Quicksilver is the chief reduction agent for extracting gold from

* See Berreyesa Adobe, Chapter 5, Santa Clara.

** State Registered Landmark #339

ore, and the discovery of gold in California had brought worldwide interest to New Almaden, the first and richest quicksilver mine on the North American continent.

In 1863 after 12 years of litigation, the Supreme Court denied the New Almaden Company's (Castillero) claim; it was the only land case in California based on a mining claim rather than a land grant. The United States was in the midst of the Civil War and eastern speculators close to President Lincoln urged him to seize the mercury-rich mine for the United States under an old law sanctioning the ejection of squatters from government land. Lincoln and his advisors were unaware that the New Almaden Company had recently purchased the Berreyesa title to Rancho San Vicente, and that the mine lay between their land claim and that of the neighboring Larios Rancho Capitancillos—the exact boundary was at that time undecided by the U. S. Supreme Court.

In July of 1863, armed with a writ of ejection, the President's agent, Leonard Swett, arrived in California with S. F. Butterworth, President of the Quicksilver Mining Company of New York, which was to operate the mine under a lease from the government. Swett and Butterworth, accompanied by the district U. S. marshal and several deputies, went to New Almaden to serve the writ and take possession of the mine. They were met at the locked gate by Superintendent Sherman Day and a band of armed men who denied them admittance. The marshal returned to San Francisco while all parties involved consulted the legal authorities in Washington and San Francisco.

At last the largely English-held New Almaden Company (perhaps with prior knowledge of the impending Supreme Court boundary decision between the Berreyesa and Larios ranchos) sold their entire holdings to the Quicksilver Mining Company for $1,750,000 on August 26, 1863. Six months later the court decision placed the hills containing the mine on the Larios property, and the reduction works and hacienda on the Berreyesa side of the contiguous dividing line running straight between the two ranchos. As the Quicksilver Mining Company already had purchased the Larios grant, the entire mining operation was finally securely held in one ownership.

Under the Quicksilver Mining Company, New Almaden became the most prominent quicksilver mine in the Western Hemisphere. The Hacienda along Alamitos Creek was developed into an attractive showplace; it was the gateway to the mines that lay in the hills a half mile down the tree-lined Almaden Road. At the hacienda was Casa Grande, the manager's imposing residence, followed by neat rows of cottages owned by the company and rented to supervisorial personnel for a nominal fee.

One of the tunnels atop Mine Hill at New Almaden.

An old brick powder house on Mine Hill above the Hacienda.

The mine and its villages flourished under the 20-year directorship of James B. Randol, who took over as general manager in 1870 when his uncle S. F. Butterworth retired. Under Randol's orderly discipline the community became a mining town unlike any other in the state, somewhat resembling a beneficent feudal society. The residents' health, wealth, cultural, and social life were taken care of by company-sponsored organizations which the progressive but authoritarian Randol set up.

After his retirement in 1892 the mine began to decline. Ore yield dropped off by more than half by the turn of the century. In 1912 the Quicksilver Mining Company declared bankruptcy and closed the mine. The hill camps became deserted with only a few oldtimers staying on in the company houses along the creek at the Hacienda. There were brief flurries of mining activity during World Wars I and II. More recently, the shafts have once again been abandoned —the mercury pollution scare having halted the last attempts to reduce the still potentially profitable cinnabar. In 1974 the County of Santa Clara purchased the hill area for development as a county park. Almaden is listed as an Historic District in the National Register of Historic Places. It also was the inspiration for the recent creation of a County Historic District Zoning Ordinance to assure preservation of the unique mining town.

Casa Grande

21350 Almaden Road

Many California towns had their "Casa Grandes," but few were more imposing than the mansion designed by General Halleck for New Almaden. It is living proof of the forgotten hamlet's past glory.

Where the Almaden road narrows to a country lane, the large, handsome house stands, marking the entrance to the old hacienda. Reminiscent of a colonial manor house, the early days of the structure are as puzzling as the remarkable man who built it.

When Captain Henry Wager Halleck assumed his duties as general manager of the New Almaden mine in 1850, he found it a primitive Mexican style mining camp. The brilliant West Point soldier took immediate steps to organize an efficient operation. Six efficient brick furnaces replaced the archaic whaling pots for reducing the cinnabar to quicksilver. By April 1852 a large range of brick buildings were erected to replace some of the old frame shelters.

Halleck visited the mine every two weeks, traveling back and forth from the office in San Francisco he shared with his law partners Archibald Peachy and Frederick Billings. Their extremely successful law firm moved to their own building in December of 1853 when Halleck's bold Montgomery Block was completed. Noted in California architectural history as the then largest building in the West it was tagged "Halleck's Folly" for its grandiose design.

Work was probably begun on Casa Grande shortly after September 1852 when Halleck's law firm filed petition in their behalf for the Castillero claim to the mine. Construction of a house and possession of the land were vital to establishing title; Casa Grande symbolized the permanency and stability of the Barron-Forbes vested interest. Halleck designed the stately three-story, 27-room building in a style that was used in much of California architecture in the 1850's. Architect Gordon Cummings, who did the final plans for Halleck's Montgomery Block may have had a hand in Casa Grande's design as well. The two buildings are somewhat similar. The fortress-like foundations, two-foot thick unadorned brick walls, and sheltered veranda with its slender wooden columns are typical of the early Italianate architecture that Halleck favored.

In 1854 Halleck resigned from the army and returned to his native state of New York to become engaged to Elizabeth Hamilton, sister of his former West Point roommate Schuyler Hamilton. Hamilton had joined Halleck at New Almaden and was left in charge as administrator while Halleck went East. Following the wedding held at the Manhattan Island estate that had once belonged to Elizabeth's grandfather, Alexander Hamilton, the Hallecks returned to San Francisco where they made their home on fashionable Rincon Hill.

Casa Grande at New Almaden's Hacienda.

Henry Halleck was never a shareholder in the mine. He was more involved in San Francisco business circles as a top land lawyer and as president of the proposed Pacific and Atlantic Railroad, although he continued to collect a $500 monthly salary as director general of New Almaden, while his law firm collected the fees for the mine's monumental legal work.

After the outbreak of the Civil War Halleck, who had distinguished himself by "gallant conduct" in the Mexican War, was commissioned Major General in the Army. Halleck visited New Almaden occasionally after his return to San Francisco from the Civil War. The mine was then in the hands of the Quicksilver Mining Company with the

former company president Samuel F. Butterworth acting as general agent and manager.

Butterworth and his wife Mary lived at Casa Grande for two years in the mid 1860's and then moved to San Francisco where their two daughters were noted "society belles" of their day. Butterworth turned over the local management of the mine to his wife's nephew, Dr. James A. Nowland, who also served as the resident physician. Casa Grande then became a chic resort hotel. Parties of the "nobs" arrived after a five-hour train and stage trip from San Francisco to spend a fortnight sitting on the broad veranda, sipping the popular Almaden Vichy Water.

When Samuel Butterworth decided to retire in 1870, he recommended his nephew, James Butterworth Randol to succeed him as general manager at New

Almaden. The young New Yorker, who had been secretary of the Quicksilver Mining Company since its incorporation, brought the then declining mine back to reach its peak production; in 1887 it paid over a million dollars in dividends to its stockholders. Under Randol's strict supervision the village became a model town. Roadways and cottages were kept trim and newly painted, enhanced with cuttings from Casa Grande's five-acre garden.

Randol also enhanced the already imposing appearance of Casa Grande. Extensive landscaping was done and the diverting of Los Alamitos Creek made a large private lake on the property. But evidently his wife Christina was never happy at New Almaden. Longing for her family and friends in the East, she left the mine in 1887 shortly after the departure of her sister and brother-in-law, the Robert Burnett Smiths. They had lived with the Randols at Casa Grande for three or four years while Smith acted as company accountant. In 1888, perhaps hoping to lure Christina and their five children back to New Almaden, Randol did a major remodeling of the mansion, putting in a gymnasium for his sons William and Frederick, and enlarging the nursery for the younger children Elizabeth and Garrey. The plan was apparently successful, for his family returned, occupying Casa Grande until James Randol retired in 1892.

Former company cashier Robert R. Bulmore then took over as general agent and moved his family into Casa Grande where they remained until the turn of the century when the famous cinnabar was thought to have been nearly mined out. When the company

General Henry Wager Halleck.

declared bankruptcy in 1912 Casa Grande was abandoned and for the next several years sat empty.

In the 1920's and 1930's the once stately mansion was used as a road-house-hotel. A variety of enterprises have been attempted here, some completely out of sorts with the home's historic past. County officials hope to raise the funds to restore the house and use it as a center for visitors to the new county park on Mine Hill.

The Carson—Perham Adobe

21570 Almaden Road

A number of historical puzzles complicate the story of the adobe building which houses the New Almaden Museum, run for many years by Connie Perham.

It is not a case of questioning whether the building is adobe or not—as is occasionally the situation where original walls have been enclosed in concrete —for the sundried adobe blocks are clearly in view.

The question seems to be whether George Carson, the *known* occupant of the adobe from 1883 to 1903, was the first telegraph operator in New Almaden (he was not—that was A. L. Bartlett in December 1877) or whether Carson was the first Wells Fargo Agent (no to that one too—that honor belonged to New Almaden storekeepers Derby and Lowe, 1887 to 1888).* Not that anyone denies that George Carson *was* a telegraph operator or Wells Fargo agent in New Almaden as well as company bookkeeper, and the postmaster in 1890.

That the Carson Adobe is of historic significance is obvious. Of the nineteen remaining company-owned employee houses it has been singled out as the one of the most historic interest. (It also is the only one of the extant three adobe houses selected for the 1937 Historic American Building Survey.) The origins of the adobes are most intriguing. When were the three adobe structures built and who first lived there?

Surveyor C. S. Lyman's map of March 1848 of Neuva Almaden, presented as evidence in the proceedings of the original Castillero mining claim marks no structures in the area. So perhaps the adobes were not built during the first building program in 1847. However, a map of September 1850 by W. J. Lewis presented in the Rancho San Vicente land case proceedings does show five structures in a row on the east side of the road, approximately where one might place the Carson Adobe (there also was a row of four structures across the road). It seems safe to assume that three of these were the extant adobes and the adobe-and-brick store (recently burned), and therefore that these were constructed sometime between 1848 and 1850, probably by the crew of Mexican workers brought to the mine in 1847 by Alexander Forbes. From land-case testimony it is known that they were making adobe bricks there during this period. A visitor in October of 1854 mentions a row of "six to eight neat cottages"—some large and handsome—the "homes of the superintendents" of the mine works, followed by the "brick yard and the cabins

---

* Information based on research done by Laurence E. Bulmore.

The Carson-Perham adobe; the photo is from the HABS files.

of the Mexican workers." The adobes might have belonged to either of these groups. One tends to support the first alternative because the original adobe structure where Connie Perham now lives is made up of three fairly large rooms arranged quite differently from the usual Californio adobes. This suggests it was built for Yankee tastes and was one of the superintendent's "cottages." Further, when Mrs. Perham moved into the house, a trellis-like breezeway was attached, which could have abetted the cottage-like appearance.

On the other hand there is a small one-room adobe standing a dozen feet away from the house. It appears to have been originally a kitchen. This typically Mexican household arrangement lends weight to arguing in favor of the adobe being one of the "cabins of the Mexican workers," but may just prove it was *built* by the Mexican workers in their usual way.

The earliest occupant whose name is on record is that of James Brodie, company bookkeeper, and in July 1861 the first postmaster and justice of the peace at New Almaden. A photograph dating from the 1860's in the files at the California Historical Society shows the adobe house with a flower laden trellis marked "At Mr. Brodie's." Since George Carson was also the company bookkeeper, it seems likely that some of the houses, frame as well as adobe, were reserved not only for management level employees but even for men of a specific occupation. The Carson-Perham Adobe may well have been the bookkeeper's residence, and when one retired, his replacement took over that particular house as well as the job.

In the 1920's, the hacienda houses were sold off by the successors to the Quicksilver Mining Company and the village came back to life as a weekend resort. Most of the cottages are still owned by families who, like Connie Perham, discovered New Almaden in those days and saved the historic mining town from total abandonment and decay.

Supplement

New Almaden

Brown shingles, lancet windows, and a gable-roof with echoing lancet inset enhance the small St. Anthony's Catholic Church, built in 1900 on Bertram Road at Almaden Road. *Across the road is the old Hacienda Hotel, which housed the unmarried mine employees and was later converted to a general hotel. Vacant for many years, it was remodeled into a restaurant.*

This fine old redwood farm house at 6468 Almaden Road *in the Almaden Valley has remained a one-family residence since it was built by Reuben Baker in 1886. When it was moved back for road widening, it was also turned to face Camden Avenue.*

"Picturesque places laid out on the gently rising
foot-hills . . . surrounded by some of the finest ranches in the county."

Mary Bowden Carroll, 1903

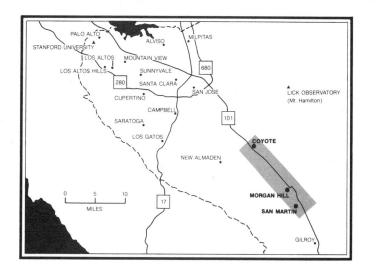

Coyote ❧ Morgan Hill ❧ San Martin

Nearly the entire history of Santa Clara County could be written by tracing the remarkable Irishman Martin Murphy and his family who came to California in 1844 in the first party of immigrants to bring wagons across the Sierra.

The towns of Morgan Hill and San Martin lay on two of the six ranchos —covering a total of over 50,000 acres —which the Murphys acquired within six years of their arrival.

Martin Murphy, Sr., a widower, was nearly 60 years old when he settled with his unmarried younger children along the Monterey Road not far from the later 21 Mile House (so called for its distance from San Jose). This roadside inn, built in 1852, became a regular stop on the Butterfield Overland Stage Line. Before that time the patriarch Murphy's adobe house was well known to early day travelers as an hospitable spot along the mission road. It stood on Rancho Ojo de Aqua de la Coche ("Pig's Spring"), which the original

grantee of 1835, Juan Maria Hernandez, sold to Charles M. Weber who in turn sold it to the Murphys in 1846. The Murphy adobe stood within the shadow of a famous south valley landmark, the 1,423-foot-high, cone-shaped peak called Oreja del Oso (Bear's Ear) by the Spaniards, El Toro by the Americans, and Murphy's Peak by the local valley folk. This peak became part of the area covered by the present town of Morgan Hill—named not for the hill but for Hiram Morgan Hill, the dashing young man who married Martin Murphy's granddaughter, Diana. Their 5,000-acre ranch was subdivided in 1892, and by August of 1893 the town of Morgan Hill boasted a post-office, church, hotel, express office, and a $5,000 passenger and freight depot.

169

Until that time the only settlements in the area had been Coyote at 12 Mile House and Madrone, both of which lay on Rancho Laguna Seca. The little hamlet of San Martin is on the adjoining Murphy rancho to the south, Rancho San Francisco de las Llagas. San Martin evolved around a chapel of that name which the devout Martin Murphy had built. Here his third son, Bernard, was buried in 1953 after his tragic death in an explosion aboard the ill-fated Bay steamer, *Jenny Lind*. The chapel lay in the vicinity of New Avenue and San Martin Avenue, two miles east of today's San Martin, which grew up later around Mills Switch Station on the railroad line.

Morgan Hill's Villa Miramonte

17860 North Monterey Road, Morgan Hill

In 1887 Carrie Stevens Walter wrote enthusiastically in a Santa Clara guide book about "Mr. Morgan Hill's neat yet spacious cottage," one of the most artistic residences in the picturesque area of Madrone. But the story surrounding the cottage is not a pleasant one.

Carrie Walter displayed ladylike restraint in avoiding mention of Morgan Hill's kinship to the notorious Sarah Althea Hill, the central figure in the sensational scandal that had rocked (and delighted) San Francisco since the story first came to public attention in the Fall of 1883.

Dan Murphy had strongly disapproved of man-about-town Morgan Hill as a partner for his diminutive violet-eyed daughter. Dan died without ever knowing about her marriage. Although the Hills were from a socially and politically important Missouri family, the popular brother and sister, both headstrong and uninhibited, were not what the wealthy stockman and his half-Spanish, half-English wife, Mary, had in mind for the Duchess of Durango, as Diana was known for her family's huge holdings in Durango, Mexico. Diana had met Morgan Hill at a fashionable resort in Santa Cruz where he cut quite a figure in his Bullock and Jones finery, driving a tandem of perfectly matched trotters. Diana was apparently as smitten with Morgan as he was with the beautiful heiress of Dan Murphy's millions. But the coy beauty played hard-to-get. Their stormy romance, which ranged from San Jose to San Francisco, was finally resolved in an

Diana and Morgan Hill's Villa Miramonte, now the Old Homestead Antiques.

impulsive elopement one afternoon at San Francisco's city hall.

The same month that Sarah Althea Hill publicized her common law marriage to the elderly financier William Sharon, her brother Morgan and his bride left their suite at the Palace Hotel for an extended trip throughout the East—probably hoping the whole mess would be over by the time they returned months later.

When they came back in 1884, the couple built this attractive six-room, summer cottage in the midst of Rancho Ojo de Aqua de la Coche, not far across the Monterey Road from her grandfather Martin Murphy's old house. Because the Hill's place was designed to view El Toro, they christened it Villa Mira Monte. The peak had always been a favorite spot of Diana's father Dan. Before his death in 1882 he often rode there to keep an eye on his huge herds of cattle.

Diana was an extremely social creature. It must have been humiliating for her as the notoriety surrounding Sarah Hill's escapades with Sharon increased and Morgan Hill's acceptance in San Francisco society suffered. By 1886, he

and Diana gave up their residence there and moved permanently to the house on the Monterey Road. Here they still lived on a grand scale—10-foot gilt mirrors, Minton-tiled fireplaces, and crystal chandeliers decorated the parlor and dining room. The double door entry on the house displayed panes of Tiffany-jeweled stained glass with the initials "MH" interlocked in the floral design. Their only child, Dianne, reportedly had her own French maid and a carriage with coachman at her disposal to call for her playmates.

Dianne eventually married a French nobleman, Baron de Reinach-Worth, but inexplicably had a nervous breakdown while on her honeymoon in France. Within months the young woman committed suicide by leaping from the window of a London sanitarium. Her mother had earlier taken up permanent residence in Paris. Her father Morgan who had done an admirable job of administering the dwindling Murphy holdings undoubtedly broke under this final blow. He turned over the 200-acre home ranch to John Holly, the ranch manager.

Diana Murphy Hill.

Then Morgan Hill, reported to be mentally ill, retired to the 25,000-acre Murphy family spread near Elko, Nevada. In November 1913 he died there on the same ranch where Diana's father Dan Murphy had passed away in 1882. Diana, "the toast of two continents," then returned from her home in France and after Morgan was buried in the Murphy plot at Santa Clara's Catholic cemetery, sold her elegant furnishings and went on to Elko.

Diana Murphy Hill never returned to California after Morgan's burial, but she did hold their home for many years. Villa Mira Monte served briefly as a funeral home. Then late in 1937 with only four acres remaining it was sold to the present owners, the Paul Waldgrens. The original stone gate posts still mark the entrance to the cottage. However, today the signpost reads "Old Homestead Antiques."

The Coe Brothers Ranch

Henry W. Coe State Park, East End of Dunne Avenue, Morgan Hill

Henry Coe Park consists of 20 square miles of mountains covered with pine, oak, and madrone, of rock-studded meadows and grassy plateaus. For centuries this hill country surrounding Coyote Gorge lay wild and unsettled. On the Historical Atlas Map of 1876 much of this land around Pine Ridge was still marked "unsurveyed."

Henry W. Coe Junior was only 16 when his father, an orchardist purchased 479 acres in the San Felipe Valley above Evergreen and established the first Coe cattle ranch. From that time on, the younger Henry Coe was first and always a cattleman. Through the years, starting in 1884, he expanded the family holdings until at the time of his father's death in 1896 they had 6,000 acres of land and more than 500 head of cattle at their ranch headquarters 3,000 feet up in the ranges around Pine Ridge.

Although after Henry Coe Senior died it was owned jointly by both Henry Junior and his brother Charles, Henry managed the ranch and lived in San Felipe Valley while Charles preferred the real estate business and lived in San Jose. They called their ranch Coe Brothers Pine Ridge Stock Ranch. A large, open-sided barn where the horses were coralled is still standing from those days. (A little ranch house dating from some years later is presently used as the park ranger headquarters.)

The cowboys of the Coe Brothers Ranch high on the Pine Ridge east of Morgan Hill.

In the 1890's The Coe Brothers Camp, a sanctuary for robins and wild pigeons in the winter, was described in the San Jose *Mercury* as stocked with cattle that thrived on the abundant native grasses—wild oats, bunch grass, and burr clover—that "cures into hay as it stands." That the Coe Brothers employed one of the most famed riders in the West, D. B. Gruell, known for his "great feats of horsemanship" was noted. An especially valuable mineral spring was also described, perhaps referring to nearby Madrone Mineral Springs at the foot of Pine Ridge. The foundations of the once well-known resort at Madrone Springs are still there hidden away in a sheltered canyon a mile or so from the Coe Corral. Henry Coe purchased the old springs and resort in 1938, which brought his holdings up to 20,000 acres according to contemporary newspapers.

Henry had long since bought out his brother's share of the Pine Ridge Ranch. He had spent 63 years developing his vast holdings. The Coe Ranch then consisted of parcels of cattle king Henry Miller's former land as well as Captain Charles Weber's Cañada de San Felipe Ranch. Although Henry Coe was semi-retired by then he still rode the range overseeing his stock. He died in 1943.

In 1953 Henry Coe's daughter Sada Coe Robinson, who inherited the ranch as part of her share of his one-and-a-half-million-dollar estate, gave 12,500 acres of the property to the County of Santa Clara. Mrs. Robinson made three stipulations to her magnificent gift. The land must be used solely for recreation, a suitable memorial to her father Henry W. Coe must be set up, and any income must be used for further park improvement.

In 1892 the "Coyote Public Hall Association" built the present Grange Hall. To the East of 101, it was moved back when the road was widened.

Boanerges R. Bailey, for whom the avenue connecting McKean Road and Monterey Highway is named, built his ranch house in 1865. It remains on Calero Creek at the end of the dam, where a levee was built to protect it in 1936, after which it was owned by Judge Edward M. Fellows. The old house is still occupied on the ranch, now run as Calero Hills Stables.

Supplement

Coyote ■ Morgan Hill ■ San Martin

Rancho Santa Teresa has had an interesting history; sadly only a few structures remain of the rancho headquarters of Joaquin Bernal, which he occupied from 1826, near the ancient fresh water spring. At **455 Bernal Road** the house of Ygnacio Bernal is made of hand-hewn timbers that appear to have been erected in the 1840's. A French saddle-maker named Changarra is believed to have used the shed on that part of the rancho at the end of Cottle Road on **Manila Drive**. If the legends are true, a stone vat at the site was used for tanning leather in the 1840's. Built over the springs nearby is a structure which served as a grotto and cave, and, in addition, as an earth-and-stone reservoir. In 1928 a shrine to St. Theresa was constructed closeby, as well as a concrete holding tank.

Not far from the Grange Hall on Highway 101 are three ranches that have existed since before old Burnett Post Office became Coyote in 1882. The well known Coyote Ranch south of **Metcalf Road** on Highway 101 was part of Rancho Laguna Seca, bought in 1845 by William Fisher, a seafaring Bostonian. Lt. John C. Fremont wintered here in 1846. The present imposing ranch house was built in the 1870's by son Fiacro Fisher. The Orvis Steven's ranch on **East Emada Lane** dates to 1867 when he bought the land. The main house was built about 1876 and has been remodeled somewhat, but a smaller house from an earlier period remains nearly intact. Stevens ran the "12 Mile House" on the road from San Jose to Monterey, where he had a store, blacksmith shop, hotel, and post office. South of the Stevens' ranch is the oldest residence in Coyote, a redwood house built by Joel Ransom in 1863. To the **west of 101** is the Joseph

Ramelli ranch, location of the 1872 Encinal School, now used as a shed. The white frame house was also built in the early 1870's.

The old Machado home at the corner of **Santa Teresa Boulevard and Watsonville Road**, now headquarters for a "tree ranch," is an 1863 structure with later additions. In front stands a redwood tree planted in 1874. Barney Machado married James Murphy's daughter Mary, thereby acquiring this portion of her father's land. His vast holdings included ranches in Baja California, that eventually equaled the land held by his father-in-law.

East of Monterey Highway, at the **end of Burnett Road**, and now part of the county's Coyote Creek Park, the Malaguerra Winery still evokes interest. A large extension was added around 1900, but the vine-covered, stuccoed stone wall of the original structure is plainly marked 1869, making it the first winery in the Morgan Hill area.

Along Monterey Road in downtown Morgan Hill there are several structures dating from the turn of the century that might be restored to expose their former characteristics. At the **corner of Third** stand the old Montgomery House on the southwest corner and Hammer's Bakery on the northeast corner, both dating from the early 1890's. At the **Second Street** corner where the furniture store is now located, once stood the old Mason and Triggs store. At the northeast corner of **Monterey and Peebles Avenue** the Madrone Hotel was built in 1895, replacing the "18 Mile House" or Madrone Station.

Looking as it did in 1893, with later additions to modernize it kept to the rear, the well maintained late Victorian Gothic Methodist Church on Monterey at 4th Street in Morgan Hill, still has the neatly prim parsonage adjacent.

On Sycamore Avenue in Paradise Valley, west of Morgan Hill and on land donated by Barney Machado in 1895, Charles Smith built a fine example of country school design for this period. A full restoration with adaptive use is planned for the old Machado School.

The very simple, modified Gothic "bird house" facade, crowned with a picturesque bell tower, remains undisturbed by later additions at the rear of the 1904 Presbyterian Church, corner of Lincoln and Spring in San Martin.

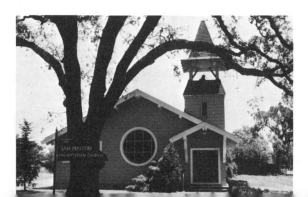

"A solid and substantially built city, with well made yet unpretentious business houses, spacious dwellings, neat cottages, green lawns, and broad and gravelled streets."

Mary Bowden Carroll, 1903

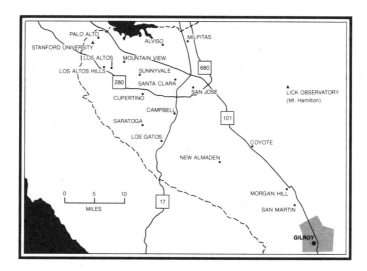

Gilroy

When 18-year-old John Cameron (later Gilroy) and his shipmate "Deaf Jimmy" were put ashore from the British ship *Isaac Todd* at Monterey in 1814, the pair would doubtless have been bemused had they known that this event would go down in the annals of California history. They were the first Anglo settlers in Alta California.

The pair made their way north along the old mission road from Monterey via Mission San Juan Bautista to Don Ignacio Ortega's Rancho San Ysidro. The young Scotsman found employment as a cooper at the little settlement that had sprung up on the Ortega rancho. Although nothing more than a random scattering of adobes, the village was a lively spot, sitting as it did near the crossroads of the trail over the Pacheco Pass and the mission road.

John Cameron, fearing that he might be returned to his ship, legally adopted his mother's maiden name, Gilroy, to avoid detection. Tall, robust, and bright, John Gilroy within a few years had captured the heart of Don Ignacio's daughter, Maria Clara. They were married and settled at San Ysidro within hailing distance of Clara's brother Quintin. Don Ignacio's principal claim to fame was his being the son of Lieutenant Jose Francisco Ortega, the renowned Portola scout who discovered San Francisco Bay in 1769, and later became commandante of the presidio at San Deigo.

The neighboring Rancho Las Animas was the domain of Don Mariano Castro, son of Joaquin Ysidro Castro, one of Anza's legendary settlers of 1776. The Castro's prominence was due in part to that distinction in addition to their apparent intelligence and gentility. (Their mother, Martina Botiller de Castro, was reputed to have been a French countess.) Rancho Las Animas was apparently the only rancho in California awarded directly by a Spanish viceroy.

177

In 1802 Mariano Castro had gone to Mexico and received a viceregal license to occupy the land with the intention of forming a settlement at La Brea, as the rancho was originally called (for the nearby tar springs). There was a subsequent boundary dispute with Mission San Juan Bautista which claimed the property, but the 26,000-acre rancho was eventually regranted to Don Mariano's widow in 1835 as Las Animas.

John Gilroy and his wife had by then inherited one-third of Rancho San Ysidro. In spite of his weakness for gambling and grog, the old Scot was named justice of the peace by Commodore Stockton after the American occupation in 1846.

When in 1850 the county officials designated which of the mile-wide wagon trails were to become dubbed "county roads," newcomer James Houck of Ohio was right on the mark with a small roadside inn and livery stable that he built on Rancho Las Animas along the San Juan and Monterey Road, a mile or so west of San Ysidro. In short order a trading post and saddler's shop followed and the town of Gilroy was born. In 1851, Houck, who reportedly could neither read nor write, became postmaster, operating from a cigar box on his front porch.

By 1868 the town was well on its way, having nearly replaced little San Ysidro (then called "Old" Gilroy). There John Gilroy, who for years had indulged his love for gambling, lived in near poverty. He had lost all of his wife's lands, herds, and possessions, but lived to see the official establishment of his namesake, Gilroy, surveyed, laid out as a city, and incorporated, before he died in July 1869.

Henry Miller, the Cattle King.

Henry Miller's Bloomfield Farm

Monterey Road, Three Miles South of Gilroy

In 1858, Henry Miller, future Cattle King of California, rode out of San Francisco where, in the eight years since landing there as a German immigrant with six dollars in his pocket, he had become the leading wholesale butcher in the state.

But Miller had bigger plans in mind as he rode southward in search of land to buy. It was an ambitious scheme to stock his own cattle on his own land, as well as butcher and sell the beef—the first step in what would become the remarkable Miller-Lux empire. Following the Mission Road down to Gilroy, then just a budding town of a dozen or so buildings, he found perfect pasture land in the hills surrounding this "Pleasant Valley," as the flatland of Rancho Las Animas was called.

Las Animas was in a complicated state of affairs, the major part having been sold off by several of the Castro heirs to Don Jose Maria Sanchez, an enterprising ranchero from San Juan Bautista. Sanchez died in 1852 without leaving a will, and his beautiful young widow Encarnacion Ortega had been married three times and widowed twice more since his death. Henry Miller was able to acquire the choicest parcel of Las Animas, held by one of Mariano Castro's daughters, Maria Lugardo. She had inherited the section that had been her father's hacienda, lying east of the Monterey Road and encircled by the Carnadero Creek. Interestingly, *carnadero* (correctly spelled carneadero) in Spanish means "butcher." The creek and tract of land around it had been known by that name for over 70 years before it became the home ranch of butcher Henry Miller.

The ranch itself, consisting of 1800 acres, had been called Bloomfield Farm by a previous occupant. By 1863 Henry Miller and his family had moved to the ranch, at first probably using Don Mariano Castro's large adobe, reputed to have been one of the finest houses in early California. A few years later,

The original 22 room house on Henry Miller's Bloomfield Farm which burned to the ground in 1923.

Castro's adobe was torn down to make way for an imposing three-story mansion in the multi-gabled style of the 1870's.

Henry and his wife Sarah were not as socially ambitious as were his partner Charles Lux and wife, who liked the city life. (She, incidentally, was Sarah Miller's aunt.) The Millers preferred living at Bloomfield. There, adjacent to the main house, Henry built an office to manage the working part of the vast Miller-Lux holdings that by 1880 covered eleven counties and 750,000 acres of land in California, Nevada, and Oregon. Never one to put on airs, Miller had close friends who were fellow stockmen and ranchers from Gilroy and Los Banos.

A Miller and Lux check dated March 5, 1879 for $5,000 in silver coin.

Bloomfield Farm, enlarged through the years to include a dairy and 10 acres of barns, sheds, bunkhouses, and harness and blacksmith shops, was where the three Miller children, Henry Jr., Nellie, and Sarah Alice grew up. In 1879, 12-year-old Sarah Alice was thrown from her horse and killed as she raced across the farm to meet her father, who returned to Bloomfield each Sunday from his exhausting weekly rounds of the major Miller-Lux cattle ranches in the San Joaquin Valley. Henry Miller never got over her death.

After daughter Nellie was married to dapper J. Leroy Nickel and living in San Francisco, and Henry Jr. married a local Gilroy miss, Sarah Onyon, the Millers spent less time at Bloomfield Farm and more time at their large home on San Francisco's Rincon Hill. Nellie Nickel's husband took an active part in the Miller-Lux enterprise after Charles Lux died in 1887.

In the northwest corner of Rancho Las Animas was a beautiful mountainous wooded area where a copper mine and old mill stood in the 1850's and 1860's. The Nickels encouraged Henry Miller to develop a summer encampment there near the summit of 1,875-foot Mount Madonna. Until the mid-1890's the Millers, Nickels, and their delighted city guests camped out in large striped tents, eating out of doors at a huge barbecue of prime Miller-Lux beef. Starting in 1896, three houses for the immediate family were built, but guests were still housed in elaborate private tents.

Henry Miller died in 1916 after a two-year illness, at the age of 89. His wife and childless son, both originally buried with Sarah Alice at Bloomfield, preceded him by several years, but Nellie and J. Leroy Nickel and their four children survived him.

In his will Miller left $15,000 to be donated at Christmas to the "Gilroy poor" (a traditional generosity he had established years earlier). He asked that he be buried at Mount Madonna, and

Henry Miller's office from the 1870's still stands on his former Bloomfield Farm.

his will provided for the erection of a burial place there. There are four or five accounts of the actual resting place of Henry Miller, the most puzzling one being that after having been buried at Bloomfield with the other deceased members of his family his casket was removed to a plot at Cypress Lawn Cemetery, then later buried in his home town of Brackenheim, Germany.

After years of litigation the Miller-Lux holdings in Santa Clara County were sold in 1926 to a San Jose real estate syndicate. Mount Madonna became a 3,000-acre county park. One of the Millers' mountain houses was brought from the summit piece by piece and reconstructed at Bloomfield Farm to replace the rambling old 22-room Miller mansion that had been totally consumed by fire in 1923. Nearby, Henry Miller's little frame office still stands on a 300-acre parcel just east of the Monterey Road, the last remnant of the once great 11,000-acre Bloomfield Farm.

Another house was brought from Mount Madonna in 1933 and reassembled on the Watsonville Road from the original lumber to appear today as it did in 1898 when it was built for Henry Miller Jr.. It can be seen today on Watsonville Road, near Day Avenue.

Fanny Stevenson's original Vanumanutagi redwood house, a miniature version of an English country lodge. The foundation stones traced with fossils were accidently placed with their intriguing designs turned inward.

Vanumanutagi—Mrs. Robert Louis Stevenson's House

Redwood Retreat Road

Five years after Robert Louis Stevenson's death in Samoa, his widow—the elfin, fiery Fanny—returned from Europe to California. She longed once again to overlook the Pacific where she and her famous author husband had spent the last years of their married life together.

Louis, as Fanny called him, had died at their South Sea retreat in 1894, at last succumbing to the tuberculosis that had racked his frail body most of his adult life. His death, inevitable, was nonetheless tragic for the strong-willed woman, ten years his senior, who had married him years earlier amidst a flurry of scandal. It brought to an end one of the great romantic adventures of their time.

They had met in the summer of 1876 at Grez, an artists' vacation colony outside Paris. Fanny, then Mrs. Samuel Osbourne, had taken her two children there during a Victorian version of a trial separation from her husband. Almost immediately a deep devotion developed between the passionate younger man and the sensuous dark beauty. Stevenson, then an unknown writer, followed Fanny Osbourne back to California where she had been living previously for several years—pursuing what he apparently sensed was a liaison of destiny. He found her in Monterey and they were married in San Francisco as soon as Fanny obtained a divorce from her reportedly philandering husband of 22 years.

In one of Stevenson's early successes, *Travels with a Donkey*, written shortly after he met Fanny, the author expressed his wanderlust. "For my part, I travel not to go anywhere, but to go. I travel for travel's sake. The great affair is to move." And move they did—at last embarking on a cruise of the South Seas that ended with their settling for a while on Samoa at a picturesque plantation they called Vailima. It was there that Stevenson died in December of 1894.

After Fanny returned to San Francisco in 1899 she engaged the renowned architect Willis Polk to design a home for her atop Russian Hill. She fashioned a model of what she wanted from matchboxes—working out a large flat roofed plan "on the Mexican order."

While the house was being built the aging, gypsy-like Fanny, invariably dressed in long, flowing blue gowns, went on a trip to a remote country inn called Redwood Retreat in the foothills near Gilroy. In June of 1900 she bought 120 acres up the canyon from Douglas Sanders, whose family owned the Redwood Retreat Inn. At first Fanny, accompanied by her Irish maid, Mary, camped out in a tent, but soon the tiny 60-year-old widow, whose grandson later claimed she was a "born architect," was designing a country cottage, again with matchboxes. It seems possible that Willis Polk assisted her in the plans for the house. Although totally unlike her San Francisco home, the structure (now completely remodeled) retains attractive features of Polk's work such as the Spanish-style front door, the simple pillars on the front porch, and fluted supports of the mantles in the bedrooms.

She hired a country carpenter, boulders from the nearby stream were gathered for the foundations, and the wooden house, a miniature version of an English country lodge, was built. She called it Vanumanutagi—Vale of the Singing Birds—a link to Samoan days. Unfortunately Fanny was not present when the foundation stones, traced with fossils, were laid. They were cemented in place with the intriguing fossil side turned inward.

Fanny, whose aspirations to artistic creativity never diminished, surrounded herself with talented people. One of her best loved friends was author Frank Norris. Fanny convinced him and his wife, Jeannette, to buy the adjoining ranch reached by a steep winding path above Vanumanutagi. He called it

Fanny in London shortly after her marriage to Robert Louis Stevenson in 1880.

"Quien Sabe." Barely had the Norris's little log cabin been made liveable, largely through Fanny's efforts, than the brilliant young man suddenly died. With the help of a couple of workmen Fanny fashioned a large circular memorial seat of stream washed stones for her dear friend. It is still there, along the pathway, as is the Norris Cabin.

In her last years the widow Stevenson's character became more bizarre. Dressed in flowing Samoan-style gowns, loaded with ornate jewelry, her hair in masses of curls and perennially smoking a cigarette, she was described as a "personage." She had become a legend even in San Francisco. A journalist is quoted as saying, "she was the one woman I can imagine a man being willing to die for." At last the little old lady's health failed and she died suddenly of a cerebral hemorrhage at her estate near Santa Barbara in February 1914. After a funeral in San Francisco her cremated remains were taken to Samoa to lie on the mountaintop beside her husband's grave.

For many years her son by her first marriage, Lloyd Osbourne and his second wife Ethel lived at Vanumanutagi. Together with his sister Belle and Ned Field, Fanny's companion, they owned nearly 300 acres near Redwood Retreat, including the former Norris Ranch. In 1935, Ethel Osbourne undertook major remodeling of Vanumanutagi for the use of her aged father. The house was thoroughly rebuilt; a second story was added, transforming Fanny's lodge into a charming mid-nineteenth century New England style house.

Chappell—Bonesio House and Winery

Watsonville Road at Day Road

When I visited the Uvas Winery a while back, I asked Louis Bonesio, Jr., why his grandfather Pietro, a native of Italy, had covered the family's historic old frame house with stucco. Louis said the old gentleman had told him that when he had the work done back in the 1930's "all the rich Dagos had stucco houses."

That probably was true enough, but it is unfortunate from an historical viewpoint because the stucco, now painted a cheerful mustard yellow, conceals all traces of the original farmhouse. From the Land Case testimony, the noted historian Dr. Jacob Bowman interpreted that the house may be on the site of a wooden house built by convict-revolutionary Joaquin Solis, who had once occupied the land and gave it his name, Rancho Solis. After his 1829 rebellion failed, Solis was banished to San Blas in Mexico and his personal effects were auctioned off at the capital, Monterey. Then in February 1831 Mariano Castro petitioned for "El Solis Rancho now abandoned and vacant." The Castro family also built a wooden house "of split logs and mud" that stood for many years in this same vicinity on Rancho Solis.

Timber from Solis' 1828 structure or Mariano Castro's of 1833 may have been used in building a small house which is incorporated in Pietro Bone-

Chappell-Bonesio House now the UVAS winery.

sio's stucco home. In 1853 Alfred Chappell, a California pioneer of 1843, moved to Gilroy township. He had traveled overland with the same party as Julius Martin, a highly respected man and one of the earliest American settlers in the area. Chappell purchased

Martin's original claim to this parcel of land and built a house.

In making repairs to the present large two-story stucco house, Louis Bonesio, Jr., found a massive 10 by 16-inch post 20 feet long running across the front part of what appears to be a second addition at the house. He also found the walls of two rooms on the ground floor dating from a very early period, built of 26-inch wide boards and hand-hewn two-by-fours. He thinks the house was originally a one-story, two-room structure, to which a second story was added in the 1860's, probably by Alfred Chappell, who lived here until at least 1885. In addition, several more rooms were added in later years on the ground floor as well as the second floor. The house was completed as it is today (in size) by Pietro Bonesio, a native of the famous wine region of Asti in Piedmont, Italy, who moved to the Santa Clara Valley in 1915. He first rented this parcel; then, in 1917 he purchased 99 acres from Barber and Company, who had operated a vineyard here before 1887. In fact, the vineyard may date back to Alfred Chappell, who was described in 1881 as one of the principal fruit growers in the area. Grapes were especially prolific in this Uvas Valley west of Gilroy. The native American Indians had come here annually from earliest times to gather the wild grapes that grew in abundance. Today's Uvas Winery consists of more than 400 acres, purchased through the years by the Bonesio family, who only recently sold the winery to a group of investors who seem to be maintaining the historic old place in good order.

Gilroy City Hall

Monterey Street corner of 6th Street

Snarled in the traffic jams that plagued this section of the Monterey Road before the Highway 101 bypass was completed, the weary driver had only one outstanding piece of architecture on which to rest his eye—the marvelously baroque Gilroy City Hall.

It was built in 1905 of sandstone blocks in a rich combination of Baroque with Mission Revival overtones. The architects were Samuel Newsom (who with his brother Joseph designed the elaborate Carson House in Eureka), plus local architects Frank Wolfe and Charles McKenzie.

The old city hall was used until 1967 and came close to being torn down. The Gilroy Historical Society has taken over its care and maintains a small museum on the ground floor of the building.

Gilroy City Hall.

Traces of San Ysidro (Old Gilroy) can still be found at the junction of Pacheco Pass Road and Frazer Lake Road. Horace Willson's home is believed to be among the oldest brick structures in the valley, the bricks having been fired on the property when the house was built in 1859. A cattleman and grocer, Willson was also the alcalde and occasionally kept prisoners overnight in his home.

An excellent restoration recently completed by Gavilan College carpentry students, is located on the campus at 5055 Santa Teresa Boulevard. The San Felipe Community Church was moved from its original location in San Benito County's "Old Dunneville" in 1972. Built in 1893, it was used by various Protestant congregations for 30 years.

Also in "Old Gilroy" the fine "stripped" Gothic-Italianate cottage with the three-story tank house adjacent is believed to be the James Phegley home built during the 1870's. The home, flanked by beautiful trees, has had excellent care.

Supplement

Gilroy

Along the Pacheco Pass Road in the San Felipe area, south of Gilroy and near San Benito County's northern border, are a number of pre-1900 structures. Situated on a knoll overlooking the valley at **4660 Pacheco Pass Road** is a rambling western house that is believed to be connected with Henry Miller, because this was "Miller & Lux" land in the 1870's when the house was built. Around 1897 Spreckels Sugar Company attempted unsuccessfully to grow sugar beets on the surrounding acres and the house may have been used as a headquarters into the early 1900's, after which time it served as a dairy ranch. At **5411 Pacheco Pass**, near San Felipe Road, the homestead of Uriah Wood may date to 1854 when he arrived in Santa Clara Valley from New York. Wood was a farmer and stock dealer who maintained 240 acres here, as well as 5000 acres in Los Banos, on the other side of the Pacheco Pass.

Off Pacheco Pass Road at **610 San Felipe Road** is "Casa del Rancho," home of James Dunne, son of James Dunne who married Bernard Murphy's widow Catherine. The home was built in 1907 on the great San Felipe Ranch that his father bought around 1860. The second story was removed about ten years ago by the present owners but the portico and columned porches remain.

South of Gilroy on **Thomas Road** is "The Homestead" built by Massey Thomas in 1853. The simple white frame house, built on a squatter's claim that grew to 1400 acres, was lived in by four generations of the Thomas family. Thomas married the granddaughter of Daniel Webster's sister and his son James is said to be the first Californian to attend Harvard University.

Northeast of Gilroy at the end of **Gilroy Hot Springs Road** the county's first spa has existed since 1865 as a tourist attraction. The proprietors guaranteed the 110° water would help cure "rheumatism, gout, lead and mercurial poisoning, alcoholism, kidney & liver troubles, bladder & urinary complaints" but added "the waters are of no benefit whatsoever to consumptives!" Developed as a family resort, the hotel with mineral baths, cottages, stables, and clubhouse was built from 1879 to 1881. The stage from Gilroy brought many notables to the spa.

The 1855 Christian Church at **160 Fifth Street**, off Monterey Road in downtown Gilroy, was relocated to the present site around 1885. Down the street on **Fifth at the corner of Church**, the Presbyterian Church has stood since 1869, a fine, simple Carpenter Gothic building, painted white and well maintained in a fine old neighborhood. Special mention must be made of the houses located on and near **Church and Fifth Streets**. Many pre-1900 homes exist in excellent condition as classic examples of their architectural styles and owners' pride.

The brick and concrete Classical Revival library at **Fifth and Church** was built in 1910 and dedicated to its benefactor, Andrew Carnegie. The land was donated by Caroline Hoxett.

As strikingly decorated as the City Hall, the 1918 Mission Revival Southern Pacific Railroad Station remains at **Monterey and Depot Streets**.

On the eastern edge of Highway 101, midway **between Leavesley and Gilman** is the farm home of pioneer Julius Martin, who brought his family overland in 1843. He operated a mill at San Ysidro from 1844 on and purchased 1222 acres west of San Ysidro in 1852 where this home is located.

Caroline Amelia Hoxett is revered for her many gifts and bequests to her adopted city. A native of Massachusetts, she arrived in Gilroy in 1868 and built this attractively detailed house soon after at 338 Fifth Street.

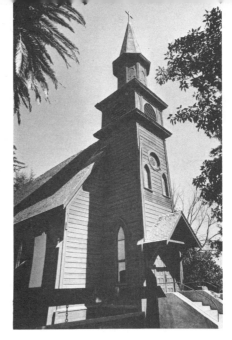

Gilroy's charming redwood Gothic Revival church, built in 1871 at 267 Martin Street must be moved soon or will be destroyed because it cannot be maintained as a church at this site.

An experienced lumberman, Logan Whitehurst built his turn-of-the-century home at 7090 Church Street, where it remains in excellent condition.

Acknowledgements

For the Junior League

In the creation of this book, we were inspired by the fine survey work and the outstanding publications of the San Francisco and Oakland Junior Leagues. And we owe special thanks to Paul C. Johnson, whose assistance over many months enabled us to complete a complex task, and to Dr. Joseph A. Baird, Jr., whose pleasure in discovering the architectural delights of Santa Clara Valley equaled our own; and to Joseph di Chiarro, who helped create something special.

In addition to those acknowledged by Phyllis Butler, we would like to thank the following: community consultants Louis Stocklmeir, Mardi Gualtieri, Melita Oden, Mary Prien, Earl E. Bowe, Al Spiers, Arthur L. Ogilvie, Leon Thomas, Jeanette Watson; the staffs of the many fine local libraries and historical societies whose collections helped immeasurably; and the numerous individuals who assisted us and whose association we treasure. Congratulations and thanks to historians Clyde Arbuckle, Lynn Vermillion, and Pat Loomis; architects Marvin Bamburg and Bruce Radde; and coordinator Thomas M. King, whose survey work on San Jose coincided with ours and was invaluable to us.

Altogether we thank the more than 25 League members who coordinated county-wide surveys, with special thanks to Virginia Sampson, whose dedication from the beginning inspired us all, and to Sylvia de Benedetti, whose request for a landmark survey by the League blossomed into a fascinating educational experience and one of the League's most exceptional accomplishments.

Historical Task Force Chairmen

Marilyn Danny Swanson, 1971–72
Carolyn Smith, 1973
Margaret Jasper, 1974–76

For the author

I would like to thank the Sourrisseau Academy for their research grant; Danny Swanson, Julie Rinehart and the members of the Junior League of San Jose who believed in the book; Dorothy Gray, Antoinette May, and Marge Sutton for technical and moral support; members and staff of the Santa Clara County Historical Heritage Commission for valuable information; members and friends of the families who built or have lived in the historic houses in this book, especially Roseanne and Bill Saussotte, Marshall Bond, and Barbara Kinchen; Birge M. Clark for the use of his memoirs; the Palo Alto Historical Association—especially Gay Woolley, Lucy Evans, and Ruth Wilson; Jean Holzclaw, Florence Fava, and Frances Fox for their helpful information; Arthur D. Spearman, S.J., for his expert help and encouragement; Jay Williar and Maude Swingle of the California Historical Society; and finally, the staff of the Bancroft Library of the University of California for their assistance in tapping the resources of this outstanding research facility.

I would like to dedicate the book to Bill, Michael, and Derek, who explored with me.

Phyllis Filiberti Butler

Pictorial Credits

Contemporary Photographs

By Gerald Fredrick: page 27, 62, 67, 76, 83, 84, 88, 94, 97, 101, 107, 116, 123, 130, 147, 171, 185, 187; in Supplement, 30T, 31T, 31B, 32T, 53C, 115B, 149T, 152T, 153BR, 155B, 175C, 188B, 189T.
By Betty Fredrick: 41B, 42, 168, 176

By other photographers: *Ed Bigelow*, 19, 20, 27, 68, 77; *Lee Foster*, 8, 156, 159, 160, 162. All photographs in supplementary sections by members of the *Junior League*, with the exception of those noted above.

Historical Illustrations

We wish to express our sincere appreciation to the following individuals and organizations that provided illustrative materials: A.A.U.W., Palo Alto, 30B; Bancroft Library U.C., 56, 60, 137, 178; Marshall Bond, 81; California Historical Society, 49, 110; Berton Crandall, 22; Mrs. Nott M. Ginsberg, 13, 44; Hoover Institution, 28; Homer Hyde, 124; Ari Kuppa, 74; Paul Masson Vineyard, 103; Reginald McGovern, 54, 63; Montalvo Assn., 104, 106; Dauphine Paine, 85; Palo Alto Historical Assn., 10, 15, 23, 16; Roger Rehm, 59; San Jose Historical Museum, 128B; Santa Clara County, 65, 181; Saratoga Historical Society, 98; Silverado Museum, 183; Charlotte Smith, 108; Mrs. T. W. Smith, 119; Stanford University, 32T, 32B, 33B; U. C. Santa Cruz, 145; Mrs. Dan Williams, 79; Winchester Mystery House, 148. All other photographs are from the author's personal collection.

Editorial Production

Executive Editor: Paul C. Johnson
Architectural Consultant: Joseph A. Baird
Designer: Joseph di Chiarro
Photographers: Gerald and Betty Fredrick
Artist: Steven M. Johnson
Copy Editor: Charles Jones
Cartographer: Josef Fellner

Bibliography

AAUW, Palo Alto. *Gone Tomorrow?* 1971.

American Architect and Builders News. 1882–1920.

Arbuckle, Clyde. *Santa Clara Valley Ranchos.* 1968.

Atherton, Gertrude. *Adventures of a Novelist.* 1932.

———— *Golden Gate Country.* 1945.

———— *Daughter of the Vine.* 1926

Baird, Joseph A. *Time's Wondrous Changes.* 1962.

Bowman, J. N. and G. W. Hendry. "Spanish and Mexican Houses in the Nine Bay Counties," Ms., Bancroft Library. 1942.

Brewer, William H. *Up and Down California in 1860–64.* 1949 printing.

Brown, A. K. *Sawpits in the Spanish Red Woods.* 1966.

———— Research notes in files of Palo Alto Historical Association.

Browne, J. Ross. "Down in the Cinnabar Mines: A Visit to New Almaden in 1865," *Harper's Magazine,* XXI (Oct. 1865).

———— *Report of the Debates in the Convention of California, on the Formation of the State Constitution, in September and October, 1849.* Washington, 1850.

Bruntz, George G. *History of Los Gatos.* 1971.

Coffman, A. D. *An Illustrated History of Palo Alto.* 1971.

Cunningham, Florence. *Saratoga's First Hundred Years.* 1967.

Cutting, T. A. *Historical Sketch of Campbell.* 1928.

Daughters of the American Revolution. *Census of 1852* (microfilm).

De Anza College, California History Center. *Local History Studies,* 21 volumes.

Division of Mines. *Bulletin 154, Geologic Guidebook of S. F. Bay Counties,* "Adobe Houses in the San Francisco Bay Region," by J. N. Bowman. 1965.

Dougal, William H. *Off for California; the Letters, log and Sketches of William H. Dougal, Gold Rush Artist,* ed. F. M. Stanger, 1949.

Egenhoff, Elisabeth A. *Fabricas.* 1952.

Elliott, O. L. and O. V. Eaton. *Stanford University and Thereabouts.* 1896.

Field, Isobel Osbourne Strong. *This Life I've Loved.* 1937.

Foote, H. S., ed. *Pen Pictures from the Garden of the World.* 1888.

Fox, Frances L. *Hakone Gardens.* 1968.

———— *Rinconada de Los Gatos.* 1968.

Garnett, Porter. *Stately Homes of California.* 1915.

Garrod, R. V. *Saratoga Story.* 1962.

Gates, Mary J. *Contributions to Local History.* 1895.

Gebhard, David, et al. *A Guide to Architecture in San Francisco and Northern California.* 1973.

Giffen, Helen Smith. *Casas and Courtyards.* 1955.

Gilroy City Staff. *Gilroy's First Century.* 1970.

Guinn, J. M. *History of the State of California and Biographical Record of Coast Counties.* 1904.

Hall, Frederick. *History of San Jose and Surroundings with Biographical Sketches of Early Settlers.* 1871.

Hannaford, D. R. and R. Edwards. *Spanish Colonial or Adobe Architecture in California, 1800–1850.* 1931.

Historic American Building Survey. *Catalog of the Measured Drawings and Photographs of the Survey in the Library of Congress.* 1941.

———— Photographic files at California Historical Society.

Hoffman, Charles. *Map of the Region Adjacent to San Francisco Bay.* 1867.

Hoffman, Ogden. *Reports of Land Cases Determined in the United States District Court for the Northern District of California (1853–1858).* 1867.

Hruby, Daniel D. *Mines to Medicine.* 1965.

Irvine, Leigh Hadley. *A History of the New California,* 2 vols. 1905.

James, W. F. and G. H. McMurry. *History of San Jose.* 1933.

Johnson, Kenneth. *The New Almaden Quicksilver Mine.* 1963.

Jordan, David Starr. *The Days of a Man.* 1922.

Junior League of San Jose. *Discovering Santa Clara Valley.* 1973.

Kaucher, Dorothy. *James Duval Phelan.* 1965.

Kennedy, H. W. and Veronica K. Kinzie. *Vignettes of the Gardens of San Jose de Guadalupe.* 1938.

Kirker, Harold. *California's Architectural Frontier.* 1973.

Landin, Les. *Saratoga.* 1966.

Lanyon, Milton and Laurence Bulmore. *Cinnabar Hills.* 1967.

Leale, John. *Recollections of a Tule Sailor.* 1939.

Lick, Rosemary. *The Generous Miser.* 1967.

Lyman, Chester S. *Around the Horn to the Sandwich Islands and California,* ed. F. J. Teggart. 1924.

Mackay, Margaret. *The Violent Friend.* 1968.

McCarthy, Francisc F. *History of Mission San Jose.* 1958.

McCoy, Esther. *Five California Architects.* 1960.

McKay, Leonard. *Early Day San Jose.* 1971.

Millard, Bailey. *History of the San Francisco Bay Region,* 3. vols. 1924.

Miller, Guy C. Notes and Collections, 1901–53. Palo Alto Historical Association files.

———— *Palo Alto Community Book.* 1952.

Munro-Fraser, J. P. *History of Santa Clara County.* 1881.

———— *History of San Mateo County.* 1883.

Neville, Amelia R. *The Fantastic City.* 1932.

Newcomb, Rexford. *Spanish Colonial Architecture in the United States.* 1937.

Newsom, J. Cather. *Picturesque Homes and Artistic Buildings of California.* 1890.

Older, Cora Baggerley. *California Missions and Their Romances.* 1890.

———— *San Francisco—Magic City.* 1961.

———— "When Santa Clara County Was Young," *San Jose News,* 1917–18.

Pallette, E. M. "Peter Coutts," *Stanford Illustrated Review,* December 1925.

Rambo, Ralph. *Local History Volumes.* 1965–1973.

Rice, Bertha M. *Builders of Our Valley.* 1957.

Rowland, Leon. *Annals of Santa Cruz.* 1947.

Sanchez, Nellie Van de Grift. *The Life of Mrs. Robert Louis Stevenson.* 1920.

———— *Spanish and Indian Place Names of California.* 1922.

San Jose Mercury Staff. *Sunshine, Fruit and Flowers.* 1895.

San Mateo County Historical Association. *La Peninsula.* Journal, 1941–65.

Santa Clara County Planning Department. *Preliminary Inventory of Historical Landmarks.* 1962.

Santa Clara Mission. *Records: Deaths, Marriages, Baptisms, 1777–1870.* Ca. 1890.

Saratoga Historical Foundation. *After Harper's Ferry.* 1964.

Sawyer, E. T. *History of Santa Clara County.* 1922.

Spearman, Arthur Dunning, S. J. *The Five Franciscan Churches of Mission Santa Clara, 1777–1825.* 1963.

———— *John Joseph Montgomery, Father of Basic Flying.* 1963.

Splitter, Henry Winfield. "Quicksilver at New Almaden," *Pacific Historical Review,* Feb. 1957.

Stanger, Frank Merriman. *History of San Mateo County.* 1938.

———— *South from San Francisco.* 1963.

Starr, Kevin. *Americans and the California Dream.* 1973.

Stuart, Reginald R. ed. "The Burrell Letters," *California Historical Quarterly,* XXVIII, No. 4, 297–322; XXIX, No. 1, 39–59 and No. 2, 173–79.

Stocklmeir, Louis. *Monta Vista and West Side Story.* 1966.

Sullivan, Sister Gabrielle. *Martin Murphy Jr., 1844–1884.* 1974.

Sweet, George E. *Index of Historical Sources for the City of Santa Clara.* 1973.

Taylor, Bayard. *Eldorado, or, Adventures in the Path of Empire.* 1849.

Thompson and West. *Historical Atlas of Santa Clara County.* 1876.

Treadwell, Edward F. *The Cattle King.* 1950.

United States, Bureau of the Census. *Census, 1860, 1870, 1880.*

United States, Land Commission. "Land Case Testimony, Rancho San Antonio, 1853–1855."

University of Santa Clara. *Diamond Jubilee, 1851–1926.* 1926.

Wait, Frona E. *Wines and Vines of California.* 1889.

Wilkes, Charles. *Narrative of the United States Exploring Expedition,* Vol. V. 1845.

Winther, Oscar O. *Express and Stagecoach Days in California.* 1936.

———— *The Story of San Jose, 1777–1869.* 1935.

Wood, Dallas. *History of Palo Alto.* 1939.

Works Progress Administration, Federal Writers Project. *California.* 1939.

———— *San Francisco.* 1941.

Wyatt, Roscoe D. and Arbuckle, Clyde. *Historic Names, Persons and Places in Santa Clara County.* 1948.

Young, John V. "Ghost Towns of the Santa Cruz Mountains," *San Jose Mercury Herald,* 1934.

191

Index

Agnew State Hospital, 93
Allen, Theophilus, house, 31
Alma College, 128
Almaden Vineyard, 102
Alviso, Don Ignacio, 56
Alviso, Jose Maria, 58
Angell, Professor, house, 31
Arguello house, 84
Baker, Reuben, house, 167
Bailey, Boanerges, house, 174
Baldwin, Charles, 109
Bayside Cannery, 57
Bernal, Ygnacio, house, 174
Berreyesa family, 77–81, 157
Berryessa, Nicolas, 57
Blaney, Charles, 107
Bloomfield Farm, 178
Bond, Judge Hiram, 82
Briones, Juana, 12, 44
Cameron (Gilroy), John, 177
Campbell, Benjamin, 124
Campbell, J. H., home, 129
Campbell, William, 95
Carson, Kit, 79
Carson-Perham Adobe, 164
Casa Grande, 158, 161
Castro, Mariano, 35, 177
Chappell-Bonesio House, 184
Church of the Five Wounds, 150
Clark, Professor A. B., 29, 31
Coe, Henry, 172
College Park, 93
Collins-Scott Winery, 39
Collins School, 114
Coutts, Peter, 15
Coyote Ranch, 174
Coyote Grange Hall, 174
Coxhead, Ernest, 52
Cribari Winery, 154
Crummey, John, house, 126
Curtner, Henry, 61
De Anza College, 111
Decker house, 30
De Saisset building, 151
Downing house, 30
Drawbridge, 67
Dunn-Bacon house, 33
Dunne, James, house, 188
Duveneck home, 49
Eaton, Marjorie, 12
Embarcadero, Santa Clara, 55
Fallon, Thomas, 137
Farley Building, 129
First Methodist Church, 149
Foothill College, 53
Foothill Congregational Ch., 52
Forbes, J. A., 58, 117, 120, 157

Forbes Four Mill, 116
Ford's Opera House, 126
Fremont, Captain John, 79
Frenchman's Cottage, 15
Garrod's Ranch, 113
Gaslight Theatre, 129
Gates, H. B., house, 153
Gavilan College, 188
German Elim Church, 93
Gilroy City Hall, 186
Gilroy Hot Springs, 189
Goodrich, Levi, 33, 142, 151
Greer, Joseph F., 26
Griffin, Willard, house, 53
Hacienda Hotel, 167
Hakone Japanese Gardens, 112
Hall, Nathan, estate, 114
Halleck, Henry Wager, 157, 161
Hanchett Residence Park, 153
Hayes Estate, 155
Henry Coe State Park, 172
Hernandez, Jose, 119
Hidden Villa Ranch, 49
Higuera, Jose, adobe, 60
Hill, Diana and Sarah, 170
Hill, Hiram Morgan, 169, 170
Hill, Morgan, 170
Hofstra Block, 126
Holy City, 128
Hoover, Herbert and Lou, 28
Hooke, George, house, 126
Hoxett, Caroline Amelia, 189
Hutchinson, Joseph, house, 31
Hyde-Sunsweet Factory, 125
Hyde, Ralph, house, 129
Interurban Railway of San Jose, 48, 96
I.O.O.F., 113, 151
Jamison house, 90
Johnson, Peter, house, 127
King, E. T., 99, 100
King, William, 100, 101, 113
Kirk, Theophilus, house, 155
Knox-Goodrich, Sarah, 151
Laine, Thomas Ashby, 66
Landrum, Andrew, house, 91
Larder house, 90
Libby, McNeil & Libby, 41
Lick, James, 86, 144
Lick Observatory, 86, 144
Lieb, Judge Samuel, 152
London, Jack, 81
Lyndon, James, 121
Lux, Charles, 179
Machado, Barney, 175
Machado School, 175
Maclay, Senator Charles, 100
Madison & Bonner Co., 41
Malaguerra Winery, 175
Markham, Edwin, house, 152
Masson, Paul, 102, 153
Maybeck, Bernard, 31, 126, 153
Maynard house, 155

McCarthy, Hannah, 97, 112
McCarty, Martin, 95, 97, 154
McCartysville, 95
McCullagh, Frank, 122
Menzel house, 92
Merriman, Isabelle, 45, 48, 146
Merriman-Winchester house, 45
Methodist churches, 112, 175
Metropole Hotel, 149
Miller, Henry, 178, 188
Mission Santa Clara, 75
Moir Building, 152
Montalvo, Villa, 104
Montebello School, 114
Montezuma Boys School, 128
Morgan, Julia, 113
Morgan, Percy, house, 53
Morse, Charles, house, 93
Murphy, Dan, 170
Murphy, Martin, 140, 169
Murphy, Martin, Jr., 35, 139
Murphy Building, 139
Naglee, Henry Morris, 152
New Almaden, 77, 135, 151, 155, 157, 167
Norris, Frank, cabin, 183
Novitiate, Sacred Heart, 127
Older, Fremont, 104, 114
Old Post Office, San Jose, 150
Osbourne, Fanny, 182–184
Pacific Congress Springs, 96
Parker, "Painless," 114
Parrish, Enoch, house, 115
Paul Masson Winery, 102
Pena, Don Jose, 72
Penitencia, 57
Peralta, Luis Maria, 133
Peralta, Sebastian, 118
Petit Trianon, 17, 109, 111
Pettis Livery Stable, 99
Phegley, James, house, 188
Phelan, James, 83, 104–108, 149
Pecchetti home, winery, 115
Pierce, James, P., ranch, 81
Polk, Willis, 107, 109, 122, 182
Presbyterian Churches, 175, 189
Presentation College, 128
Price, Eliphalet, house, 129
Professorville, 18, 31
Purissima School, 53
Quaker Meeting House, 92
Quicksilver Mining Co., 158
Ramelli, Joseph, ranch, 175
Ranchos, 12, 16, 49, 57, 60, 78, 84, 95, 107, 118, 135, 136, 140, 174, 177, 178
Rengstorff, Henry, 36
Richardson-Theurekauf home, 155
Riker, W. E., "Father," 128
Robert-Sunol Adobe, 135
"Roundhouse," 152
Rucker house, 154
St. Anthony's Church, 167
St. Joseph's Church, 150

St. Stephen's, Gilroy, 189
St. Thomas Aquinas Church, 30
Sainte Claire Club, 149
San Antonio School, 114
San Felipe Church, 188
Sanford, Fernando, house, 18
San Francisco-San Jose Rr., 50, 56
San Jose Historical Mus., 151
San Ysidro (Gilroy), 188
Santa Clara Co. Courthouse, 141
Santa Clara Mission, 75
Saratoga Foothill Club, 113
Saratoga Paper Mills, 100
Schultheis, John, cabin, 128
Scott, E. W. and Angelia, 40
Seale, Thomas, and Alfred, 23
Shoup, Guy, 52
Shoup, Paul, 43, 48, 52
Smith, J. G., house, 52
Solis, Joaquin, 184
Sorosis Fruit Packing Co., 113
South Bay Yacht Club, 67
South Pacific Coast Railroad, 55, 57, 67, 118
Southern Pacific, 48, 90, 152, 189
Springer, J. P., house, 112
Squire, John Adam, 21
Stanford University, 32–33
Stevens, Elisha, 108
Stevens, Orvis, ranch, 174
Stevenson, R. L., Mrs., 182
Sullivan's Saloon, 150
Sunol, Don Antonio, 155
Sunsweet Factory, 125
Toll House, Los Gatos, 126
Thomas, Massey, house, 188
Tilden-Laine House, 65
Townsend, J. H. M., farm, 152
Trinity Episcopal Church, 149
Troy Laundry, 152
Union Warehouse, 67
University of the Pacific, 93
University of Santa Clara, 75
Uvas Winery, 186
Van Reed, James and Julia, 46
Verein, Santa Clara, 90
Villa Montalvo, 104
Wade, Charles E., house, 67
Wade, Harry, 62, 63
Warburton, H. H., house, 92
Weller, Joseph R., 57, 61
Whitehurst, Logan, house, 189
Wilbur, Ray Lyman, home, 33
Willow Glen, 155
Willson, Horace, house, 188
Winchester, Sarah, 45, 48, 127, 146; House, 146
Wolfe and Wolfe, 153
Wood, C. A., house, 112
Wright, William, house, 41
Zanker, William, house, 67